Derbysh

Derbyshire

COUNTRYSIDE BOOKS
NEWBURY BERKSHIRE

First published 2004
© David Bell 2004

COUNTRYSIDE BOOKS
3 Catherine Road
Newbury, Berks

To view our complete range of books,
please visit us at
www.countrysidebooks.co.uk

ISBN 1 85306 868 3

Designed by Peter Davies, Nautilus Design
Produced through MRM Associates Ltd., Reading
Printed by Woolnough Bookbinding Ltd., Irthlingborough

CONTENTS

INTRODUCTION 7

1. **FRED GREAVES** 9
   - the first Derbyshire man to receive the Victoria Cross

2. **ALICE WHEELDON** 14
   - radical feminist and pacifist

3. **RON PETERS AND TOM LEWIS** 18
   - cavers and potholers

4. **JOAN WASTE** 26
   - 16th-century Protestant martyr

5. **NIGEL VARDY** 30
   - rock climber who survived the horrors of a
   snow storm on Mount McKinley in Alaska

6. **ALISON HARGREAVES** 35
   - climbed Mount Everest alone

7. **WILLIAM MOMPESSON AND THOMAS STANLEY** 37
   - heroes of the 17th-century Eyam plague

8. **HAROLD LILLY** 42
   - Japanese prisoner of war

9. **ERIC WALTON** 46
   - member of Lord Mountbatten's and
   General Browning's war staff

10. **FLO SIDDONS** 50
    - a grandmother who fought for justice

11. **GEORGE LOWE** 57
    - member of the 1953 expedition to Mount Everest

CONTENTS

12. BESS OF HARDWICK . . . .**.59**
  - the second most important woman in
Elizabethan England

13. DENNIS SKINNER . . . .**.65**
  - Labour politician labelled 'the beast of Bolsover'

14. BRIAN CLOUGH . . . .**.71**
  - manager of Derby County Football Club 1967–1973

15. JOSEPH PAXTON . . . .**.76**
  - head gardener at Chatsworth House

16. ELLEN MACARTHUR . . . .**.81**
  - the sailor from Whatstandwell

17. CATHERINE BOOTH . . . .**.89**
  - 'mother' of the Salvation Army

18. JOE PAYNE . . . .**.96**
  - the stuff of football legends

19. JOSEPH WRIGHT . . . .**.99**
  - 18th-century painter

20. PHOEBE BROWN . . . .**.104**
  - Derbyshire's strongest woman

21. JACK BODELL . . . .**.106**
  - British Heavyweight Boxing Champion

22. BARNES WALLIS . . . .**.111**
  - inventor of the bouncing bomb

23. PETER FIDLER . . . .**.115**
  - 18th-century surveyor

24. JAMES BRINDLEY . . . .**.120**
  - canal builder who 'chained the seas together'

BIBLIOGRAPHY . . . .**.125**
ACKNOWLEDGEMENTS . . . .**.126**

Introduction

I hope you enjoy reading this book about Derbyshire heroes, some of them well known, others who ought to be. Not enough people have heard of Peter Fidler, the Bolsover man who became the chief mapmaker to the Hudson Bay Company, or even of Joan Waste, a young blind girl, burned at the stake for having religious beliefs that did not coincide with those of the ruling queen.

The collection is deliberately eclectic. All the people included in the book are heroes to some Derbyshire residents, although I'm sure that everyone who reads this book will, at some point, come across one of my heroes that they do not rate. Those who appreciate finding war heroes like Fred Greaves VC and Lt Col. Harold Lilly may disagree with the inclusion of Alice Wheeldon, Derby's famous conscientious objector, framed on a charge of trying to assassinate the prime minister in 1917.

With sporting heroes, choosing whom to include is even more contentious, though I cannot imagine anyone disagreeing that Ellen MacArthur is a Derbyshire hero. Jack Bodell, who brought the British heavyweight boxing championship to Derbyshire, is another choice I hope might prove popular, and also Joe 'Ten-Goal' Payne, who deserves to be better known than he is.

And as for including a politician, oh boy! That might raise some eyebrows. On the other hand, Derbyshire people of all party allegiances respect this particular man, and he challenges his own leaders as much as his opponents. Bess of Hardwick is another controversial choice, since she achieved power and wealth through her four marriages. However, considering that she did it in the Elizabethan era, when women rarely got the chance to achieve anything that wasn't purely domestic, her determination must have been on a heroic scale. Formidable! That same Derbyshire grit and determination can be seen in the grandmother who fought for 18 years to bring her grand-daughter's killer to justice.

I hope everyone will agree with the inclusion of those brave people who are part of the cave rescue service. There are mountaineers, too, including a young man who went back to climbing after losing his fingers and toes to frostbite, and a young woman who tragically lost her life on K2, after becoming the first woman to climb Everest without the aid of oxygen or porters. There are figures from the county's history, too: the painter known as Wright of Derby; Joseph Paxton, Chatsworth's famous gardener; James Brindley, the canal pioneer; and Sir Barnes Wallace, the inventor of the bouncing bomb. I have included William Mompesson, of Eyam plague fame, and have tried to give equal prominence to Thomas Stanley, whose part in the Eyam events tends to get overlooked.

You will also find in these pages Eric Walton, a miner's son who had an extraordinary war; Phoebe Brown, Matlock's strong woman, who could 'break in a horse better than any man'; and Catherine Mumford of Ashbourne, whose strength lay more in the moral field. She went on to found, with her husband, William Booth, the Salvation Army. Even if you disagree with one or two of my choices, I hope you will find plenty to enjoy.

David Bell

1

Fred Greaves

- the first Derbyshire man to receive the Victoria Cross

Fred Greaves was born on 15th May 1890 at Killamarsh, and was the oldest of twelve children. He left school at 13 and became a coalminer, working at Barlborough no. 2 pit of the Staveley Coal and Iron Company Ltd. When he was in his late teens, there was a serious accident in the coalmine, resulting in Fred breaking both of his legs. He spent two years in Chesterfield hospital, and, when he came out, the doctors advised his father to buy him a bicycle to help to strengthen his weakened legs. This must have been a sound suggestion, since Fred went on to join the Sheffield Wheelers Cycling Club and even won three gold medals for cycling. In 1914, Fred was the Derbyshire 50-mile and 100-mile cycling champion.

That same year, like thousands of others, Fred and his brother Harry went to volunteer for service in the army. Harry was accepted and went on to become a captain in the Sherwood Foresters, the regiment staffed by men from Derbyshire and Nottinghamshire, but Fred was turned down because of the earlier injuries to his legs. However, he tried to enlist again, a year later, and this time he was accepted, becoming a private in the 9th Battalion of the Sherwood Foresters.

In October 1917, Fred, now an acting corporal, found himself at a place called Poelcappelle, in Belgium, taking part in the terrible battle of Passchendaele. This battle lasted three and a half months, from 31st July until 17th November, and was unbelievably costly in terms of lives lost. Frequently, in appalling conditions, a small area of land was gained, only to be lost again the next day. When soldiers went 'over the top', they exchanged the mud of the trenches for machine-gun fire pouring towards them from the enemy gun emplacements. Some 60,000 British and Commonwealth servicemen lost their lives in the mud and bullets of Passchendaele. Many of those who survived described it as an apocalyptic experience, a vision of Hell. And yet during the carnage there were soldiers who behaved with superhuman courage.

On 4th October, Fred Greaves found himself in a potentially fatal position. As his company advanced towards a German concrete pillbox, four machine guns opened up, slaughtering many of the men. All of the officers and senior NCOs were either killed or injured, and the soldiers wavered, unsure whether to go on or retreat. Fred ran on, dodging the bullets, and managed to get to the pillbox. He threw in his hand grenades, and the pillbox was captured. For his bravery under fire, he was awarded the Victoria Cross, becoming the first Derbyshire man ever to be given that distinction. His actions on that day were described in the London Gazette as follows:

'For most conspicuous bravery, initiative and leadership when his platoon was temporarily held up by machine-gun fire from a concrete stronghold. Seeing that his platoon commander and sergeant were casualties, and, realizing that unless this post was taken quickly his men would lose the barrage, Corporal Greaves, followed by another non-commissioned officer, rushed forward, regardless of his personal safety, and reached the rear of the building and bombed the occupants, killing or

capturing the garrison and taking four enemy machine-guns. It was solely due to the personal pluck, dash, and initiative of this NCO that the assaulting line at this point was not held up and that our troops escaped serious casualties.'

The courage shown in the action described would surely have been enough to last most men for a lifetime, but that was not the end of Fred's brave exploits that day. The Gazette continued:

'Later in the afternoon, at a most critical period of the battle, when the troops of a flank brigade had given way temporarily under a heavy counter-attack, and when all the officers of his company were casualties, this gallant non-commissioned officer quickly grasped the situation. He collected his men, threw out extra posts on the threatened flank, and opened up rifle and machine-gun fire to enflade the advance.'

Thus, on two occasions on the same day, the Derbyshire coalminer, initially turned down for the army because of the injuries to his legs, proved himself a man of outstanding bravery and a born leader of men. It is no wonder that the Gazette report concluded:

'The effect of Corporal Greaves' conduct on his men throughout the battle cannot be over-estimated, and those under his command responded gallantly to his example.'

Fred was later promoted to the rank of sergeant.

When Fred was demobbed, he went back to Barlborough to resume life as a coalminer. He was a modest man, enjoying his hobbies of gardening and fishing. His brother Harry worked down the mine, too. Fred's daughter Hazel tells one amusing story of Harry shouting to Fred, 'You want to clean that dirty medal!' This jest was overheard, and the

Fred Greaves, seated, and his brother Harry

outraged listener was only prevented from reporting the comment when Fred explained that no one was insulting him or his VC; it was only his brother pulling his leg.

Another of Hazel's stories concerns an occasion when Fred and his wife were invited to a garden party at Buckingham Palace. As their taxi approached the palace, the taxi driver asked which entrance he should head for. 'Any entrance will do, I think,' Fred told him. The driver turned round to say something and saw Fred putting on his medals. 'That's the Victoria Cross,' the impressed driver said. 'We're definitely going in the main entrance, mate!'

Fred carried a bullet embedded deep in the back of his thigh for many years after the war. Then, one day as he climbed into a coal wagon at work, he winced. His workmate looked up in amazement when Fred said, 'Ouch! That's my bullet.' The man laughed, thinking it was a joke, until Fred explained that it really was true. The bullet had worked its way towards the surface of his skin and Fred was able to go to Chesterfield hospital and have it removed. It had been in his leg for 36 years.

Harry Greaves, who had himself been awarded the DSO, Military Cross and two bars, had suffered from a gas attack during the war and died at the age of 52. Fred died at Brimmington at the age of 83, after a full and happy life. In July 2003, Hazel Greaves was invited to tea with the Mayor of Chesterfield, and she tells me that she is pleased that photographs of her father and his medals are to be put on display in the Mayor's Parlour. In his will, Fred left his actual Victoria Cross to the Sherwood Foresters museum, though Hazel was given a replica. Hazel says that her father was 'a lovely man' and she is very proud of him.

Although Fred Greaves was Derbyshire's first VC, the same award – the top military medal – was made to two further Derbyshire soldiers the following year. Charles Edwin Stone of Ripley, a bombardier in the 83rd Brigade of the Royal Field Artillery, gained a VC in March 1918 and Company Sergeant William Gregg of Heanor, serving with the 13th Battalion of the Rifle Brigade, was awarded the VC two months later.

2

Alice Wheeldon

- radical feminist and pacifist

Some of the heroes in this book fought in the First World War and committed their acts of heroism on the battlefield. Alice Wheeldon, on the other hand, was a socialist, a convinced atheist, and an ardent opponent of the war. She lived at 12 Pear Tree Road, Derby, where she ran a shop selling second-hand clothes.

As a radical feminist, she had been a member of the Women's Suffrage Movement, but had been outraged when the movement's leaders decided to support the war. Alice's son William had been imprisoned as a conscientious objector at the beginning of the war, and, by 1916, Alice was using her own home as a safe house for conscientious objectors and deserters. Also living in the house was her daughter, Harriet, an elementary teacher. Another daughter, Winifred, was married to a laboratory assistant and lived in Southampton.

The safe house in Pear Tree Road had come to the attention of the authorities, and information had been passed to the intelligence section in the Ministry of Munitions, a department which later became MI5 and the Special Branch. One of the men using Alice's home as a shelter from military service was Alec Gordon, and he introduced another man into the household. The new lodger, known only as Comrade Bert, told Alice that he was a member of International Workers of the World and an army deserter.

ALICE WHEELDON

In fact, both men were government agents sent to infiltrate the Wheeldon family. Comrade Bert was Herbert Booth, and Alec Gordon was in reality E. Vivian, a former journalist turned secret agent whose identity the government was anxious to keep secret.

Alice Wheeldon and her family were keen to raid a camp where conscientious objectors were being held prisoner. Comrade Bert pointed out that it would be necessary to kill the camp's guard dogs and suggested that Alice should approach her son-in-law to obtain suitable poisons. Alice agreed, and wrote to Alfred Mason, asking him to obtain both curare and strychnine from the laboratory at Hartley University College in Southampton, where he worked.

Alfred and Winifred shared Alice's view of the war, and in January 1917 four phials of poison were dispatched from Southampton to Derby. They never reached Alice Wheeldon's address, however. They were intercepted by the authorities, who, of course, knew all about them. Alice and Harriet Wheeldon were arrested in Derby, Alfred and Winifred Mason in Southampton. The charge against them was not of plotting to raid the detention camp, but, incredibly, of conspiracy to murder the prime minister, David Lloyd George, and his minister Arthur Henderson! It was alleged that the strychnine and curare were to be used on darts to be thrown or fired at the two men.

At the trial of the four members of the Wheeldon family, the prosecution team was led by the Attorney General, Sir Frederick ('F.E.') Smith. He was assisted by two KCs, a junior barrister, and a host of expert witnesses, including the leading pathologist of the day, Bernard Spilsbury. In contrast, the defence case was put by one barrister, Mr Riza, and one solicitor. It was never going to be an even contest, and the trial lasted only 30 minutes.

Mr Riza, who claimed to be related to the Persian royal family, was somewhat eccentric. At the beginning of the trial he asked that the four accused should undergo trial by ordeal, referring to the medieval practice of prisoners undergoing some form of physical ordeal such as walking over hot coals; the Almighty, it was believed, would protect the feet of the innocent! What the firmly anti-religious Alice Wheeldon made of her lawyer's ludicrous suggestion was never recorded.

The prosecution based much of its case on the character of Alice Wheeldon and her family. They were, it was stated, militant atheists who had once burnt down Breadsall church, though no evidence for this allegation was produced. Moreover, Alice was a supporter of women's suffrage and had known of a previous plot to murder Lloyd George by driving a poisoned nail through the sole of one of his boots.

Most of the letters written by Alice to her son-in-law had referred to needing poison to kill the guard dogs at the detention camp. However, the letters produced in court were ones in which the dogs were not mentioned. The only witness called was Herbert Booth, 'Comrade Bert', who gave evidence that Alice had told him of the plot to kill the prime minister and Arthur Henderson. Booth's employment by the intelligence service was not mentioned.

Three of the family, Alice, Albert, and Winifred were found guilty, and Harriet was freed. Alice Wheeldon was sentenced to ten years in prison, Alfred Mason to seven years, and his wife Winifred to five years. Her sentence was lighter, the judge commented, because she had obviously been influenced by her wicked mother.

Throughout the trial, the judge, Mr Justice Low, had been appalled by Alice's swearing in court, commenting that, as members of the Wheeldon family were teachers, it must follow that elementary education of the general public was a bad idea. Alice had refused to compromise in court. While denying that she had ever plotted to murder, she remarked that she thought Henderson was a class traitor, and the country would be better off if Lloyd George's career came to an end. She added that 'George at Buckingham Palace' was another man whom the country could do without.

It is highly possible that the prime minister became aware that the whole trial had been a farce, based on dubious evidence from government agents. In 1919, he ordered a review of the case, and Alice was released. However, her time in prison had been marked by hunger strikes and violent forced feeding, and she lived for only a few weeks after her release. She was buried in an unmarked grave in Derby, but her legend lives on. A television version of her story was shown in 1983, with Brenda Bruce playing the role of Alice, and a play, *The Friends of Alice Wheeldon*, written by Sheila Robotham, was first performed in 1988.

For many, Alice Wheeldon is one of the greatest heroes Derbyshire ever produced. Her commitment to the causes of pacifism and feminism is indisputable, and her moral and physical courage can only be admired.

3

Ron Peters, Tom Lewis and Others

- cavers and potholers

Cavers and potholers are a unique breed of people. They pursue their hobby – though for many of them it is more a way of life than a hobby – in a subterranean world that would terrify the non-caver. We may think of a cave entrance as a large hole in cliffs or hillsides, but many caves are entered vertically from a small crack in the ground. Once in a cave, how many of us would happily squeeze through a narrow fissure to discover what was on the other side? Or duck below water where the cave roof descends to meet the surface of an underground lake, hoping to come up in another chamber? To many of us, this is the stuff of our worst nightmares.

For the dedicated speleologist, however, the exploration of caves and underground tunnels is the most rewarding and fascinating activity. A caver needs to be physically and mentally fit, and knowledgeable about the skills and techniques connected with caving. He or she must also be aware of what can go wrong, because caving is a hazardous pursuit. Risk can be minimized by careful planning and carrying the correct equipment, but nevertheless an element of danger is always present.

There are people who complain that those who go down caves are putting themselves in unnecessary danger and that others should not be expected to rescue them. I disagree. For some, life without any risk would be a flat and boring existence, and it is these very people whom we always call on in time of peril to help us. If a caver does get into trouble, it will be other cavers – all volunteers – who will come to his rescue. Mind you, if the rescuers think that the person they have helped out has been foolish or ill prepared, they will certainly let him know; a blistering expletive-laden reprimand from an experienced caver would leave you in no doubt of your folly!

One Sunday afternoon, in March 1959, a group of climbers from the British Speleological Association were exploring Peak Cavern near Castleton. This cave, known locally by the picturesque name of *The Devil's Arsehole,* has a large and imposing entrance portico, which once contained a rope-works and some cottages. Thousands of visitors, including school parties, go into Peak Cavern every year. Once away from the tourist parts of the cave, however, it does contain some challenging routes in its inner depths. The whole cave system runs for more than ten miles, and includes areas named the Devil's Staircase, Squaw's Junction, the Trenches, Mucky Ducks, and Pluto's Dining Room.

The BSA party climbed up a wet and muddy passage on their hands and knees into a high, level chamber. Up on the wall was the entrance to a narrow shaft, discovered only two weeks earlier. They knew that the shaft was tight and that it corkscrewed. Neil Moss, a 20-year-old Oxford student, volunteered to make the first descent, and 75 feet of flexible ladder was lowered down. Neil began the descent, kicking the surplus ladder before him. The shaft dropped 12 feet, and led to the difficult corkscrew, followed by an almost horizontal bedding plane, and then a further ten-foot vertical shaft. It was like a giant S-bend. Neil managed the first drop and inclined plane but experienced difficulty in the second drop, when the ladder beneath him became jammed with loose boulders. He decided to ascend, to let someone else have a try. He called up to tell the others he was coming up, but ten minutes later he hadn't appeared, and his colleagues realized something was wrong. One man went down and discovered that Neil was in a shaft only 18 inches wide and was unable to lift his feet enough to use the rungs of the ladder. The others tried to pull up the ladder with Neil Moss on it, but he became jammed. He had also become exhausted. To add to his discomfort his lamp went out, possibly through lack of oxygen, leaving him in complete darkness.

After several attempts to pull him up with a rope, which broke each time, two of the men left to fetch outside help. It was now two hours since Neil Moss had gone down the shaft, and he was in serious trouble. The slight airflow that had been passing through the shaft was now blocked by his own body, and he was becoming disorientated. The man who had been on the inclined plane just above him had to leave, suffering from a severe headache.

At 7.30 pm, a 14-strong party from Leicester Art College, who had been exploring a different part of Peak Cavern, joined them. They gave what assistance they could, but by 8.30 pm it was obvious that the situation was desperate. Two of the cavers went off to try to obtain an oxygen bottle. The oxygen bottle arrived at 12.30 am and was lowered down towards the trapped man, with its valve partially open.

Finally, the police were asked to call out the Derbyshire Cave Rescue Organization and five members of the Orpheus Caving Club were summoned from Derby. None of the five had a phone, and the Derby police had to visit each house. Two of the Orpheus members were Tom Lewis and Ron Peters. Tom recalls, 'The first I knew about the rescue was a

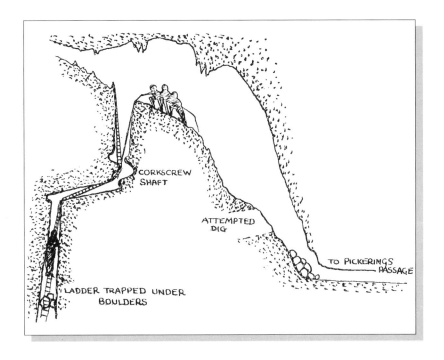

The attempted rescue of Neil Moss. (Jim Eyre)

knock on the back door late on Sunday night.' It was the police, who told him he was needed to take part in a rescue in Peak Cavern, and that transport would be along shortly. That turned out to be a Black Maria, which turned up at 1.30 am, causing some rumours among the neighbours until they found out where he had really gone! Tom was the last to be picked up, and he had to be the navigator for the 45-mile journey in thick fog. He recalls that the police driver, who had been on duty for 14 hours, did really well to get them there in one piece.

Tom took over the organizing of food and equipment, while Ron Peters and the others joined the rescuers. Ron

Peters managed to get down to the trapped student and fastened a rope to him, but it broke again. The RAF mountain rescue team from Harpur Hill was also present, and Flight Lieutenant Carter, a doctor, devised a method of getting oxygen to the men attempting to descend the shaft towards Neil Moss. This was fairly makeshift: a long rubber tube was attached to the oxygen bottle, and the man making the descent had to carry the other end of the tube between his teeth. When Tom Lewis tried the descent, he began to black out and had to be pulled back up. To this day he does not know whether his problem was caused by foul air or by the opposite: too much oxygen. Ron Peters made repeated attempts to go down again, but in vain.

The next morning, Monday 23rd March, other cave rescue teams who had heard of the situation via news bulletins on the radio turned up to offer their help, but all that could be seen of the unfortunate caver was a mud-covered blockage far below. It was reported that he was immovably trapped with one arm through the rungs and jammed into a recess. An attempt – more in desperation that in hope – was made to tunnel through to a spot below the man, but this soon hit solid rock.

Eventually, Neil Moss stopped breathing, and when word came that constant rain was causing the Mucky Ducks area of Peak Cavern to flood, the rescuers were forced to make a reluctant withdrawal. This was the first time the cave rescue team had failed to retrieve a comrade, and they all felt a sense of sadness and failure. A few weeks later, Tom Lewis returned to the location. He placed wood and rocks over the shaft where Neil had died, and a companion chiselled the name of the dead caver on the wall, together with the year. Unfortunately, the man was not a good speller, and the inscription actually reads '1959 NIEL MOSS R.I.P.'. Cavers have given the name 'Moss Chamber' to the area above the shaft where Neil Moss's body still lies.

One good thing to come out of this tragedy is that liaison between the various rescue teams and related organizations in Derbyshire and surrounding counties has greatly improved.

The following August, Ron Peters was awarded the George Medal, while Ft Lt Carter and two other rescuers, Les Salmon and John Thompson, were awarded the British Empire Medal. All the awards were well merited, though it is also true to say that every caver who took part in the attempted rescue, including a 16 year old girl, was a hero. In my eyes, all cave rescue members are.

In his wonderful book, *Race Against Time*, Jim Eyre, a caver

Epitaph carved above Neil Moss's final resting place. (Graham Foster)

with over 50 years of experience who was present at the failed rescue, states: 'The Neil Moss tragedy is a classic example of how a seemingly trivial occurrence underground can lead to disaster. Inexperience, faulty equipment, and failure to recognize and act effectively upon a serious situation all played a part. Lack of co-ordination amongst the emergency services and the general circus-like atmosphere at Peak Cavern with the press creating their own 'heroines' and 'heroes', even to the extent of dragging a circus acrobat out of retirement, were balanced by individual acts of heroism of many of the underground workers who tried in atrocious conditions to rescue the stricken youth.'

Neil Moss was not the only caver to get stuck in that vicinity, and is not the only one to have given his name to a feature there. Graham Foster, a member of the British Speleological Association, was present at the attempted rescue of Neil Moss in 1959. About four years later, he and his companions were back in the same location. They had crawled along Pickering Passage, past the Neil Moss Chamber, and were engaged in clearing out mud and rocks from a blocked shaft. Nearby was a small chamber about six feet by two, which could be reached via a narrow entrance passage about ten inches in diameter. There were strange howling sounds coming from the chamber, and Graham decided to investigate. He crawled through the narrow entrance passage into the chamber and found that at the far end there was a crack about an inch wide, with running water on the other side. It was the running water that had been the cause of the weird noises.

Curiosity satisfied, Graham attempted to go back. The chamber was too small for him to turn round, so he had to back along the ten-inch entrance tunnel. 'Unfortunately,' he told me, 'there was a step up from the chamber to the tunnel, and I just couldn't get my feet up high enough. I was stuck!' He was also very well aware of the fate of Neil Moss, entombed not too far away. Luckily, he was able to shout to his comrades still working nearby. They enlarged the entrance, and, after slipping out of his protective 'goon' suit, he was eventually able to back out to safety. 'For many years,' Graham says, 'that ten-inch tunnel was known by cavers as Foster's Folly. It probably still is. Embarrassing, really.' Graham later went on to become a cave rescue leader, himself.

———◆———

4

Joan Waste

- 16th-century Protestant martyr

Joan and Roger Waste were twins, born in Derby in the year of 1544, during the reign of Henry VIII. Their father, William, was a ropemaker and barber.

It was soon realized that Joan had been born blind, and in her childhood it was her brother Roger who would lead her about the streets in the parish of All Hallows, where they lived. All Hallows' church would later become the Derby cathedral of All Saints. Joan never let her blindness stop her from being active. She would help her father with his ropemaking and also learned to knit stockings, which brought her a small income.

As she grew up, Joan became interested in religion, which was, of course, of the Protestant variety, given the influence of the monarch. She found that she could feel her way to all the Derby churches, and managed to attend a service every day. She listened to the sermons and Bible readings and could soon repeat them from memory. Her great wish was to own a Bible of her own, and eventually she saved enough money to buy a copy of the New Testament.

Although her blindness meant she was unable to read it, she would persuade her brother or other friends to read it to her. One of these readers was John Pemerton, the parish clerk of All Hallows' church, and another was John Hurt, an elderly inmate in the local prison, where young Joan Waste used to visit with food. Hurt was an educated man, who had been imprisoned for debt. He looked forward to Joan's visits and enjoyed reading to her. Joan grew up a deeply religious Christian, whose quiet but determined faith was one of the things that was admired by the local Derbyshire people.

Then, miles from Derby, an event took place that was to have a tragic effect on the life of the young blind girl. Edward VI, the boy king who had inherited the throne after the death of his father, Henry VIII, died at the age of 16. He was succeeded by his eldest sister, Mary. Queen Mary was an ardent Catholic who hated the Protestant religion which her father had introduced into England. Overnight, everyone – clergy and laity alike – had to change their religious practices. When Protestant bishops were executed, most people found that they could make the required change back to Catholicism. Those who stuck to their Protestant opinions learnt to keep their heads down and outwardly to conform.

Back in Derby, Joan Waste was now 20 and living with her twin brother, following the death of their parents. She was an honest young woman and found it impossible to deny her religious beliefs. This came to the notice of a Derby official named Peter Finch, who reported Joan to Rafe Baine, the Bishop of Lichfield. The bishop sent for Joan while he was visiting Derby, commanding her to attend All Hallows' church and submit to being questioned.

The question that caused her the most trouble was that of transubstantiation. This tenet of the Catholic faith insists that the wine taken at mass literally turns into the blood of Christ and the bread into his body. As a Protestant, Joan could not accept this, insisting that the bread and wine were only symbolic of blood and flesh. Today, this disagreement might seem rather abstract, but in the 16th century, these were important matters of state. Under Queen Mary, Joan's views were heretical, and heresy was punishable by death.

Also present at the bishop's questioning of Joan were Sir John Port, Henry Vernon, Peter Finch, and Dr Draycott, the bishop's chancellor. The blind girl bravely stood by her beliefs, saying that the wine and bread were representations; she even said that the wine and bread at the Last Supper were not literally changed, quoting learned scholars on the subject. Some of the authorities she quoted had already been put to death for their views; so she was playing with fire. Dr Draycott, in particular, was outraged by her behaviour, although the bishop was reluctant to put what he called 'this poor, blind, unlearned woman' to death.

At one point, a situation arrived that could have saved the girl's life. Joan said that if the bishop 'would take it on his conscience, that the doctrine which he would have her believe concerning the sacrament was true, and that on the dreadful day of judgement he would answer for her therein, she would then further answer them'. The bishop was pleased and began to answer that, indeed, he would. He was, however, interrupted by the much more ardent Dr Draycott, who icily told him, 'You do not know what you do. You may in no case answer for a heretic.'

The chance had gone, and Joan was imprisoned for four weeks and then brought into church on 1st August 1566 to be publicly denounced by Dr Draycott, who stated that she was morally as well as physically blind. He ordered her to be burnt to death, saying that, just as her body would be destroyed by fire, her soul would burn in Hell for all eternity.

Joan accepted her fate with quiet courage and was led from the church by her grieving brother. He supported her as she was taken to Windmill Pit, where the bonfire was waiting. The young Derby woman said goodbye to her brother and then said her prayers as she was tied to the stake and the fire was lit. Joan died a truly horrific death by fire, rather than give up her faith. Bishop Blaine was genuinely troubled by the event, but Dr Draycott, despite saying that he was in sorrow for her death, retired to an inn and slept soundly during the execution.

In the Protestant–Catholic strife, the cruelty and intolerance was not all one-sided. During the later reign of Elizabeth I, it was three Catholic priests from Derby – Nicholas Garlick, Robert Ludlam, and Richard Simpson – who were put to death for refusing to convert to the new official religion. All were brave, but – perhaps because of her gender, her youth, and her blindness – it is Joan Waste who is remembered in Derby as a martyr and a hero. People think of her courage as she died in the flames and the bravery of her devoted twin brother, who had to lead her to her fate and watch her die.

———◆———

5

Nigel Vardy

*- mountaineer who survived the horrors of a
snow storm on Mount McKinley in Alaska*

Nigel Vardy lives in Belper, and he says that one of the
best things about his school – Belper High School –
was that one morning a week was spent on outdoor
pursuits. There was rock-climbing, caving, and sailing. At
that time, Nigel had no interest in climbing, and he usually
opted for sailing. In fact, whenever Nigel saw climbers
dangling from ropes – a common sight in Derbyshire – he
thought they must be mad. Although he never fancied
mountain climbing, he liked adventure, including hill
walking in all weathers.

When he left school, Nigel became an apprentice cable
jointer with the electricity board, and, in 1994, he took
three months' unpaid leave to go on a Raleigh International
expedition to Chile, spending his time there studying the
country and the people. In subsequent years he worked in
Guyana and Bolivia, although on these occasions he was
able to take his annual leave consolidated into a month's
holiday each time. Nigel says that his first inclinations
towards travel and adventure were probably inspired by
watching the Indiana Jones films and reading about warfare
in foreign parts, with the love of mountain climbing coming
some years later.

It was in Chile that he did his first rock climb, virtually by
accident. Trying to take a photograph of some local

parakeets, he pursued them up a rocky waterfall. The climbing bug gradually claimed him, and in Bolivia he was thrilled to ascend to the summit of Illimani, 21,000 feet above sea level.

Then, at the age of 30, he went with fellow-climbers Tony Hollingshead and Steve Ball to climb Mount McKinley in Alaska. At 20,320 feet, McKinley is North America's highest peak. It was May 1999, and the three men had been having the best seventeen days' climbing of their lives on West Rib, a particularly challenging route up Mount McKinley. On the eighteenth day, a Wednesday, a severe snowstorm hit the three climbers, causing Nigel to suffer severe frostbite in his left eye. The powerful wind took the temperature down to −60°C; so Nigel, Tony, and Steve took shelter in a crevasse. At one stage, Steve Ball began to suffer from hypothermia, and his two companions huddled together with him to share their body warmth. They managed to send out a radio message for help before the radio was dropped 100 feet, rendering it useless.

Meanwhile, unsure whether their mayday call had got through, Steve Ball, now partially recovered from his hypothermia and the least frostbitten of the three climbers, had decided to leave Nigel and Tony and go off for help. Steve, at 42, the oldest and the most experienced climber, was trying to descend to the ranger camp 5,000 feet lower down, but he was still at 18,000 feet on the Denali Pass when he fell, breaking both legs.

The Denali Park rangers had received the radio message but all they could make out was that three climbers were injured somewhere above the 19,000 feet level. The high winds and severe weather conditions prevented an aerial search for the injured men, but, just before midnight, the weather cleared and emergency supplies including another radio were dropped from a helicopter close to where the men were believed to be sheltering. Nigel and Tony turned on the new radio and heard the rangers saying that they would be back for them in fourteen minutes. That estimate was amazingly accurate, Nigel recalls, and he and Tony were located and rescued.

They were flown to hospital in Anchorage early on the Friday morning. Nigel was suffering from severe frostbite to his face, feet, and hands. Tony was treated for a shoulder injury, and frostbite to his feet and hands; he sustained the least permanent injuries, losing the tips of only three fingers.

A party of five climbers, including a Canadian doctor, found Steve Ball the following afternoon. He was flown to Anchorage, suffering from dehydration, hypothermia, and an open fracture of his leg. Steve lost all his fingers and thumbs, half his left leg, and part of his right foot. He has since been fitted with an artificial hand.

Nigel Vardy says that the cold had frozen his fingers and toes, turning them harder than stone. He recalls them staying black and dead for weeks. 'Watching your body die before your very eyes is an incredible experience,' he says. 'There is nothing you can do but pray that it will end. All my life I wanted to do something different, go to strange places, and do unusual things. Now, I just wanted to be my old uninteresting and complete self again.' All his toes were amputated, and today he jokes that he once wore size nine climbing boots but now takes a size five (left) and a size six (right). He also lost most of his fingers, being left with only short stumps. His nose had to be remodelled, using skin grafts from his forehead.

It might be thought that these injuries would have cured Nigel Vardy of his urge to climb, but not so. A year later, he was back rock climbing at Harboro Rocks in the Derbyshire Peak District, before tackling the near vertical Chere Couloir and conquering the Allalinhorn in the Alps. The year 2002 found him tackling the 21,000 feet Island Peak in the Khumbu region of Nepal, and in 2003 he went to North America to attempt Tête Blanche, the highest mountain on Baffin Island in northern Canada.

When I spoke to Nigel at his home in Belper, he told me that after his injuries he had difficulty even standing up. He says he knew he had to learn to walk before learning to climb. He speaks movingly of the difficulties he experienced while re-mastering skills he had originally learned as an infant: standing up, walking, holding a toothbrush, using a knife and fork. He points out that an adult brings to the tasks psychological and emotional baggage in the form of frustration, depression, and an overwhelming feeling of *why-can't-things-be-like-they-were-before*. At his lowest point, he even wondered whether he would be better off dead. But this gutsy young man fought on with determination and courage. He recalls the joy of seizing a pen late one evening and managing to write out all his feelings and hopes. He wrote long into the night, covering eleven pages with his writing.

Eventually, Nigel went back to climbing and mountaineering. He admits that he is not now the climber he was before, finding rock-climbing particularly difficult, though he says that he manages well on ice. His finger stumps are weaker than his fingers were, and more inclined to bleed, and he finds it necessary to tape them up while climbing. However, it was his lack of toes that proved the biggest problem. He found full mountain boots more useful than rock climbing boots, as their solid construction compensated for the fact that the front of the boots contained no toes!

Nigel Vardy, back climbing again in 2001.

He loves mountaineering, but confesses that it does cause him physical pain and, although he likes to travel, Nigel comments that he is always delighted to come back to Derbyshire. 'It is a very special county,' he says.

For me, Nigel Vardy's real heroism lies not so much in the height of the peaks he has climbed – though that is brave enough – but in the way he had refused to let his terrible injuries stop him from doing what he enjoys most: climbing mountains all over the world. He has not just conquered summits, he has conquered his physical and psychological demons.

6

Alison Hargreaves

- climbed Mount Everest alone

One of Derbyshire's most famous mountaineering heroes was Alison Hargreaves. Like Ellen MacArthur, she was born in Whatstandwell, which raises the question of how one Derbyshire village can produce two such outstanding young women, one a sailor, the other a mountaineer!

Alison was only the second person to climb Everest alone, without the aid of either oxygen or Sherpas. Since the only other climber to have achieved that feat was Reinhold Messner, Alison was obviously the first woman to do so, and the first Briton. She had previously attempted the climb in 1994, but, at 27,500 feet, had been driven back by arctic winds. She was only 1,500 feet short of the summit but was in danger of suffering severe frostbite to her feet and hands.

She tried again in 1995, and, using the notorious north ridge from Tibet, she got to the top of the world's highest mountain just after midday on Saturday 13th May. She was 33 years of age, only 5 feet 2 inches tall, and so slight that she was a size eight dress size. At the summit, the first thing she did was to radio her base camp, asking them to send a fax message to her two children, six-year-old Tom and four-year-old Kate, who were at home with their father in Fort William. She expressed her elation at being at the world's highest spot and dedicated the climb to Tom and Kate.

After a two-week break in Scotland, Alison challenged

herself once more by climbing K2, the world's second highest peak, again without oxygen or porters. She reached the peak on 13th August, exactly three months after her triumph on Everest, but tragedy struck soon afterwards. Alison and three of her companions were killed when a sudden storm brought a 100 mph wind. Peter Hillary, the son of the first man to climb Everest, was on the same expedition but had not attempted the summit, and he survived. The following year, Jim Ballard, Alison's husband, took their young children to Pakistan on a pilgrimage to the foot of K2, to see the mountain where their mother had died.

Instead of celebrating the accomplishments of Alison Hargeaves, some of the press began to turn nasty, criticizing her for leaving her two children. She was accused of being irresponsible for combining the duties of motherhood with the activities of mountaineering. This seems outrageous to me. We never criticize women who go into other dangerous professions – firefighters, police officers, etc. – whether they have children or not. We rightly admire their courage and dedication. And would the same criticism apply to male climbers with young children? I doubt it.

Alison Hargreaves was what she was: a brave and committed mountaineer. She was also a caring and loving mother. Which other climber has ever celebrated a success by radioing a message to his or her children from the very summit?

Her husband Jim, a climber and photographer, commented: 'Everyone has the right to live their own lives. How could I have stopped her? I loved Alison because she wanted to climb the highest peaks her skills would allow her to. That's who she was.'

7

William Mompesson and Thomas Stanley

- heroes of the 17th-century Eyam plague

The Reverend William Mompesson was appointed rector of the Derbyshire village of Eyam in April 1664. He was a young man with a wife and two children. He had only been in that post for a year, when a terrible plague hit the village, and villagers began to die a horrible death.

An itinerant tailor, George Viccars, was lodging with the Cooper family in Eyam, and in early September 1665 he received a box containing textiles and clothing from London. When the box was opened, the contents were found to be damp and so the tailor laid them out in front of the fire to dry out.

Within a few hours, George Viccars became ill. He took to his bed, but the next day he was worse, and three days later he was dead. His symptoms had been horrifying: swellings on his neck and in his armpits; purple blotches on his chest; severe vomiting; and a high fever, followed by shivering and sneezing. He was the first victim of what became known as the Eyam plague. It is thought that the clothing in the box sent from London contained live rat fleas and that these fleas carried the bubonic plague, which had been rampant in London that year. Now it was in the Derbyshire village. George Viccars was buried on 7th September in the village churchyard.

The second victim was Edward Cooper, with whom the tailor had been lodging, and in the next few days four of Cooper's neighbours had died the same painful death. A

The window in the church at Eyam tells the story of the plague
(Eyam Parochial Church Council)

further 23 villagers died in October, but only seven in November. As the hard winter set in, it seemed as if the plague had been defeated. People began to hope that the freezing Derbyshire weather had wiped out the terrible affliction, but, when spring came, that hope was dashed. In June 1666, 16 more died, and people began to despair.

Most of the wealthier folk, including Squire Bradshaw, had left Eyam to stay with relatives elsewhere. Someone had to take charge, to prevent panic setting in; the two men who did so were the young rector, William Mompesson, still in his twenties, and the former Puritan minister, Thomas Stanley. Although Stanley, a widower, had been removed from office in 1660, with the restoration of the monarchy, he had remained in the village and was held in high esteem. William Mompesson and Thomas Stanley forgot their religious differences and worked together for the common good.

The first thing they did was to prevent any more public funerals and burials in the churchyard. Each family was now instructed to bury their dead in their own gardens or out on the hills. The village church was permanently locked and services were held outdoors, in a location known as Cucklet Delph. Finally, and most drastically, villagers were forbidden to leave Eyam. The epidemic was to remain in the village and not spread through the neighbouring villages.

William and Thomas marked the village boundary with stones and stakes, and everyone was honour bound to remain within. The self-imposed isolation of Eyam was reinforced by the nearby towns of Bakewell and Tideswell, which employed men to watch for refugees from Eyam and drive them back to their own village with rocks and stones. Most of the inhabitants of Eyam did remain within the village bounds, however. People from nearby villages would bring them food and clothes and leave them outside the village. The people of Eyam would pay for the goods by leaving the money in a trough of water and vinegar, in the belief that the vinegar would disinfect the coins.

The last Eyam victim of the plague was buried on 1st November. The epidemic – and the isolation of Eyam – was over. The survivors burned bedding, furniture, and clothing and fumigated their homes, before beginning their lives again. Prior to the plague coming to Derbyshire, the population had been 350; during it 259 people died and 75 families were affected. One of those who died was Catherine Mompesson, the beloved wife of the rector.

It cannot be denied that the actions of both William Mompesson and Thomas Stanley were heroic, as were those of all the unselfish villagers. Nevertheless, part of me does wonder whether those residents of Eyam who watched their children die ever resented the fact that William had sent his own children away, before he persuaded them to agree to the self-imposed quarantine.

Like William Mompesson, Thomas Stanley survived the plague. He died in Eyam in 1670. William Mompesson left the village to re-marry and take up a living in Eakring in Nottinghamshire. It may be that Eyam held too many sad memories for him. Every year, his heroism is remembered in a religious service held in the open air at Cucklet Delph. For some reason the name of Thomas Stanley, the co-instigator of the heroic stand at Eyam is less renowned.

The plague itself is remembered in the children's rhyme:

> Ring o' Ring o' Roses
> A pocket full of posies.
> Atishoo! Atishoo!
> All fall down.

The tomb of Catherine Mompesson in Eyam churchyard. (David Moorley)

The *ring o' roses* refers to the purple blotches that appeared on the chest of plague victims, while the *pocket full of posies* was the bunch of flowers and herbs carried to ward off the disease. *Atishoo* represents the sneezing phase of the fatal illness, and *all fall down* is a jocular reference to victims dropping down dead.

8

Harold Lilly

- Japanese prisoner of war

Lieutenant Colonel Harold Hutchinson Lilly commanded Fifth Sherwood Foresters in Singapore, but he became famous among all the regiments and prison camps in the Far East for the courageous manner in which he stood up to the Japanese camp authorities. He always spoke up on behalf of his men, often taking beatings for things they were alleged to have done.

Harold Lilly was born in Sitwell Street, Spondon, in 1893. He served as a captain in the First World War, during which he was captured and interned in Holland. After the war, he was promoted to major, and in 1934 he became a colonel, in charge of a battalion. A year later, he left the army to work as a director of a firm of Derby printers, Bemrose & Sons. In 1938, the 45-year-old colonel was recalled to military service and posted first to France and then to Malaya.

When Singapore fell to the Japanese, he and his men were captured and forced to march through the jungle, covering 85 miles in six days. When one man dropped dead of exhaustion, the Japanese commandant insisted that the rest continued with the march. Colonel Lilly pointed out that the men were suffering from blisters and were in no condition to march. The outraged commandant said that he could have the colonel shot for refusing to obey his orders, but Harold Lilly replied that they had better shoot him there and then because his men were not going to march. He won this psychological battle; the prisoners were allowed to recover before resuming the march.

The battalion was taken to a prison camp at Wampo (or Wang Po) in Siam (now Thailand), which eventually held 1,500 men. The prisoners were made to construct a length of railway line with a viaduct and bridge at each end. This was to form part of the 250 mile line being built from Ban Pong in Siam to Ye in Burma, the notorious 'death railway'. In prison camps on each side of the Burma–Siam border, there were nearly 62,000 prisoners of war, all forced to work on the construction of the railway. Of these, 30,000 were British, the others being Dutch and Australian, plus a small number of Americans (about 700).

The work was incredibly hard, and to say that the prison conditions were extremely poor would be an understatement. Cruelty was commonplace and deprivation was everywhere. The prisoners worked for sixteen hours a day, and slept 24 to a ten-man tent or fifteen in a bamboo hut measuring fifteen feet by six feet. As their clothing wore out, many were left wearing rags or only a loin cloth. All of the men lost much of their body weight, and 20% of the prisoners were to die of disease, exhaustion, or ill-treatment.

The food was mainly rice and salted dried vegetables, in small quantities. Colonel Lilly made repeated representations to the Japanese authorities, and the camp at Wampo became the first to get a meat ration. The amount of meat was miniscule, the prisoners having to supplement it by catching lizards and snakes, but the point had been made. It was another psychological victory for the colonel.

One reason put forward for the cruelty of the Japanese military towards their prisoners is that the concept of prisoner of war was alien to the Japanese warrior code.

Soldiers were expected to be victorious or to die; anything else was viewed as dishonourable. It is remarkable that Colonel Lilly forced his captors to review that ingrained attitude.

After the war, the battalion padre, the Rev. E. Nesling, commented that Colonel Lilly 'often took punishment from the Japanese because he was always furthering our cause for additional food and so on'. Medical supplies were also in very short supply, and the padre described occasions when Lt Col. Lilly suffered brutal assaults from the Japanese whilst trying to obtain clandestine medicines for the men 'from local Siamese sources'.

Because of his bravery and the manner in which he put the morale and well-being of his men before his own health, Colonel Lilly became a legend throughout the camps. He was the inspiration for the fictional character of Colonel Nicholson, played by Alec Guinness in the film *Bridge on the River Kwai*. It is often noted that Alec Guinness did have a close physical resemblance to Harold Lilly, but all the men who survived the camp agree that the fictional colonel differed in one major respect from Harold Lilly: while he became obsessed with building a perfect bridge for his captors, Colonel Lilly was devoted solely to the welfare of his men. Colonel Lilly was very strong-minded, and, despite being physically at the mercy of the Japanese, he was able to stand up to them. He was later to say, 'I was able, shall we say, to outwit the Japanese with whom I had to deal. Where we could get the upper hand, we made fairly reasonable camps.'

Padre Nesling said, 'I cannot speak too highly of the successful efforts made by Colonel Lilly on our behalf. By reason of his forceful personality, he soon had the Japs in a comparatively amenable frame of mind. I am sure that his efforts in those early days in the jungle were responsible for saving many lives.' Captain W.F. Thirlby, another officer who was in the death camp with him, wrote, 'The highest praise is due to Col. Lilly. He has done magnificent work for the Foresters and for all the men who have been with him in Siam. The people of Derby should be very proud of him.'

When Harold Lilly returned to England after the war, his first comments were typically not about himself but about his men. 'No words of mine,' he said in 1945, 'can praise sufficiently the conduct of the other ranks, whose spirit was never broken, even in the darkest hours.' Although he had received many beatings at the hands of his Japanese captors, even they came to have respect for the English colonel. On the back of a photograph sent to Colonel Lilly by a Japanese major-general in September 1945 are the surprising words: 'To express my cordial friendship'.

Colonel Lilly never married. He returned to Spondon, living in Dale Road, but his health never really recovered from the conditions of the death camps. He died at the age of 61 in 1954, nine years after the end of the war, and was given a military funeral. Having no family, he left his house in Dale Street to his devoted housekeeper, Anne Longdon.

Bridge on the River Kwai is universally regarded as a classic war film, but it is the real heroism of Lieutenant Colonel Harold Lilly, not the fictional obsessive character of Colonel Nicholson, which is remembered by the people of Derby. One of his greatest Derby admirers tells me, 'Although Colonel Lilly received an OBE for his work in the prison camps, many of us feel that he should have been given the Victoria Cross.' It is certainly true that Harold Lilly's heroism in the death camps of Burma and Siam is as remarkable as the heroism of those who displayed it on the field of battle.

9

Eric Walton

*- member of Lord Mountbatten's and
General Browning's war staff*

Eric Walton is another man who had an interesting life during the 1939–45 war, though much of it was necessarily secret. Eric, the son and grandson of a miner, lived in Hepthorne Lane, between North Wingfield and Clay Cross, south of Chesterfield. At about the age of twelve, Eric learned to write shorthand, taught by a man named Nelson Turner, who, Eric thinks, may have been a reporter. Eric left North Wingfield Elementary School at the age of fourteen, and worked as a confidential clerk, first at Shipton Halliwell, a firm of solicitors, and then at Hardwick Colliery. He attended Chesterfield Technical College three days a week, studying for a National Certificate in Commerce. In 1937, he had a serious accident; he was knocked off his bicycle and injured his pelvis.

When he went for a medical for military service with two of his friends in 1939, Eric was classed Grade 2 because of his injury, unlike his friends who were classed A1 and enrolled into the army. Two or three years later, Eric was called up into the RAF and was posted to RADAR HQ in Leighton Buzzard, which he describes as a very hush-hush place. When, as a young married man, he was posted abroad, he had no idea where he was going when he left from Liverpool. He soon realized that he was going via the Mediterranean and through the Suez Canal. Eventually he arrived in India and was sent to New Delhi. Eric was amazed to be introduced to Lord Mountbatten, the newly appointed Supreme Allied Commander in Asia.

Lord Mountbatten called his new staff together, all men of different specialities, and addressed them. Much of the information was top secret, but Eric tells me that Mountbatten was a great believer in the importance of communication. He always let his staff know what was going on. He told them that they were the advance echelon, and said that Churchill had ordered that the Japanese, who had overrun Siam and Burma, were to be kept out of India. If India could be kept safe, then the counter-attack could be launched into Burma.

Corporal Eric Walton found that he was working for Philip Mason, the head of the Indian Civil Service, and was surprised to discover that he, too, was a Derbyshire man, from Duffield. At this time, Philip Mason would attend meetings and then dictate the minutes to Eric immediately afterwards. Mountbatten moved his headquarters to Ceylon, appointing General Sir Fred Browning, the husband of Daphne du Maurier, as his chief of staff. Eric Walton was promoted to sergeant and seconded to the staff of the general.

In August 1945, Philip Mason told Eric that he was to accompany him to Rangoon to meet a delegation from Japan. They were to arrange a ceasefire in Burma, and Eric was to make a verbatim record of the negotiations. Eric felt that he didn't have sufficient skills to do this, but, when he voiced his doubts, he was overruled. The authorities had more confidence in his competence than Eric himself.

They travelled to Government House in Rangoon. To Eric Walton it looked like a film set, with lights and film cameras everywhere. The Japanese general Numata Takazo surrendered to the Allied forces and thanked General Browning for allowing the Japanese officers to wear their swords during the negotiations. The talks took place in a large room, and the three plenary sessions took three hours. Sergeant Eric Walton took shorthand notes throughout, and, at the end of each session, he was put in a side room to draft the minutes.

After the ceasefire in Burma, American General MacArthur negotiated another ceasefire in the Pacific and Eric found that he was part of the official delegation invited to go to Singapore to witness the official signing of the surrender of the Japanese in September 1945. It was an impressive occasion and it marked the end of the war. However, General Browning commented to Eric, 'Sergeant, I don't know what all the fuss is about because we did all the hard work in Rangoon!'

After the war, Eric still had a year's RAF service to complete. He was appointed confidential clerk to the staff of Lord Killearn, the former British Ambassador to Egypt. They were based in the sultan's palace in Johor Baharu, but travelled throughout the Far East to Saigon, Bangkok, Shanghai, and Hong Kong. In August 1946, Eric was invited to stay on but decided that he would rather return to his wife and home in Derbyshire. He went to work in Bolsover and became the Area Secretary of the National Coal Board.

Amazingly, Eric was never asked to hand in the books containing the shorthand notes he took at the Japanese surrender in Rangoon. He brought them home with him after the war, and in 2003 he handed them over to the Derbyshire Records Office in Matlock, along with other photographs and documents. The county archivist, Margaret O'Sullivan, stated, 'Eric Walton's collection will be kept as a discrete archive. Every item will be catalogued and

Sgt Eric Walton, Sgt Dawson, and General Browning in conversation.

preserved where necessary, and will be available for the public to see.'

Eric is very modest about his wartime activities. 'After all,' he told me, 'my friends down the pub are hardly going to be impressed if I admitted that I spent the war as a shorthand writer, are they?' I think they might be impressed if he were to mention some of the things he witnessed and some of the people he worked with, but Eric is not a name-dropper. He claimed he only came to work for Lord Mountbatten and General Sir Frederick Browning because he could do shorthand, but I think his proven qualities of reliability and discretion might have had more to do with it.

10

Flo Siddons

- a grandmother who fought for justice

Although some readers may imagine that an avenging angel should be tall, dressed in white, and carrying a flaming sword, I think that she could be five feet tall and speaking with a Derby accent. Some of Derbyshire's heroes achieved that status through acts of courage in situations they went into willingly. Flo Siddons is a hero, because for eighteen years she showed determination and steadfast courage in a situation that no one would like to contemplate. When her granddaughter Lynn was murdered in 1978, Flo pursued her killer for nearly two decades, until he was finally brought to justice.

Lynn was actually 'granny-reared', in that Flo and her husband, Fred, brought her up. She regarded Flo and Fred as her parents, though she knew that her big sister, Gail, was actually her biological mother. Back in the early 1960s, single parents were less accepted than today. In close and caring families, it was common for a family to accept the new baby and for its grandmother to rear the child as her own.

It was Flo, with her strong sense of right and wrong, who went round to confront the father of the baby, a married man who lived on the same estate, and give him a piece of her mind on the subject of getting her 16-year-old schoolgirl daughter into trouble. Flo was a battler even then.

In 1978, Lynn left school at Easter and had a family holiday with relations in Italy. She was due to start work at the Co-op but still had the Easter holidays to enjoy. On Easter Monday, she was expecting her boyfriend Bobby to take her to the fair, but she wasn't sure whether he would come to pick her up in the afternoon or the early evening. When he hadn't arrived by mid-afternoon, she decided to go round to a neighbour's house to see her friend Roy. Roy Brookes was fifteen, only a year younger than Lynn, but he looked and acted like a 12-year-old. Lynn was quite protective of Roy, and stood up for him when other children on the Sinfin estate called him names. She liked his mother, Dot, but found his stepfather, Mick, a bit creepy.

That afternoon, Lynn and Roy went for a walk, as Roy had told her he wanted to go to a farm where they might give him a part-time job. As the two teenagers left, Mick Brookes watched them walk down Carlyle Street and then turn off towards Red Woods. Lynn never returned from that walk.

When Flo and her other daughter, Cynthia, came home from shopping, Lynn wasn't at home. They knew she couldn't be too far away because her purse was still there and she hadn't left a note, something she always did if she was going to be away for long. When Flo enquired at the Brookes' house, Roy was at home, claiming that Lynn had gone off while he was in the wood having a wee. Flo found this odd, since open fields surrounded the wood, and, even if Lynn had decided to go somewhere on her own, Roy should have been able to see her.

By 10 pm, Flo and her worried family called the police. Their reaction to the news that a 16-year-old girl who had a boyfriend and was hoping to go to the fair was missing on a bank holiday was to tell the family not to worry. Lynn was probably with her boyfriend; she would come home when she was ready. Flo, who obviously knew her granddaughter better than the police, found this scenario unlikely. At 2 am,

Flo Siddons, the grandmother who battled for justice.
(Derby Telegraph)

Flo's two sons took torches and a dog and searched Red Wood, but they found nothing.

In the days that followed, the police questioned young Roy Brookes, who now said he saw a white car in the area where Lynn had disappeared. Mick Brookes annoyed Flo by making comments about the missing girl's sex-life, comments that she knew were untrue. Still the police refused to take the case seriously, and the Siddons family took things into their own hands. Firstly, they made copies of Lynn's photograph and took them to the fair, asking people if they'd seen the girl. When this didn't produce results, Cynthia went to her MP's surgery and asked him to get involved. The MP was Philip Whitehead (now an MEP), a former journalist and television producer. He was appalled that nothing was being done and approached the local newspaper. The Saturday edition of the *Derby Telegraph* carried a front page spread about Lynn's disappearance. Flo Siddons learned at this early stage that if the authorities are not doing enough, the only answer is to do it yourself.

Lynn's body was discovered on the Sunday, by the towpath of the Trent and Mersey canal. A post-mortem showed that she had suffered multiple stab wounds, some very superficial, but others penetrating four inches into her body. She had also been strangled by someone standing behind her. Roy Brookes was taken into custody, but wept continuously, refusing to answer questions. The police were getting nowhere with him and made the decision – wrongly, as it turned out – to allow his stepfather ten minutes alone with him to calm the boy down. After this conversation, Roy Brookes told the police that he had stabbed Lynn because she had taunted him. Roy was charged with the murder. It seemed that no one had even wondered how a slight young boy could have subdued and killed a much bigger, fit, strong girl like Lynn.

At his trial, Roy Brookes told a different story. He said that his stepfather had told him to take Lynn for a walk, and had followed them. Along the towpath, Mick had grabbed Lynn from behind, and produced a carving knife. He had ordered the boy to stab Lynn. He was so terrified that he obeyed, though he did it gently so as not to hurt her. Roy managed to break the knife blade, but his stepfather produced another knife, plunging it deep into the girl's body. The jury could see that this was the most likely scenario and that Roy Brookes alone could not have committed the killing. They took only twenty minutes to acquit him of murder.

To the astonishment and distress of Flo and her family, however, Mick Brookes was not arrested and charged. He just went home – and his home was only a few doors away from the Siddons' house. This situation went on for some years. Flo knew who had killed her granddaughter, but he remained free. Remembering the earlier lesson, Flo's family took action themselves. Petitions were circulated, marches were organized, and Mick Brookes was hounded, first from Sinfin and then from his new home in the city centre.

Flo would set off for work early and then stand silently outside Brookes' house for fifteen minutes every day. Other people were more direct. His windows were broken, and graffiti was painted on the door. In 1980 – two years after the murder – Flo's daughter Cynthia was charged with trying to run down Michael Brookes with her car. The charge of attempted murder was reduced to one of dangerous driving, and she was fined £100 with £300 costs. The Siddons family had no compunction about their vendetta. They knew Brookes was guilty of murder and he was getting away with it. The police continued to say that there was insufficient evidence to charge Michael Brookes. At one stage, Brookes made the considerable error of leaving his wife, Dot, who made a statement to the Siddons' solicitor, saying that her husband had confessed to murdering Lynn Siddons. However, when her husband came back to her, she withdrew the statement.

In 1981, the campaigning journalist Paul Foot became involved. Paul – probably better known for acting on behalf of the wrongly convicted – thought it outrageous that the police were doing nothing in the case when the whole of Derby knew the identity of the killer. He used his *Daily Mirror* column to review the murder, using the reckless driving case as his lead-in, and he named Michael Brookes. He also gave Flo Siddons the name of a young solicitor, Jane Deighton, who might help her. Jane came up with what seemed an outrageous suggestion. Flo and her family should sue Michael and Roy Brookes in a civil court for damages for Lynn's death.

There were many problems with bringing the case, one judge ruling that it should have been brought within three years, but eventually his ruling was overruled. The main problem was raising the money for the case. Flo Siddons had strong principles and would not allow a public appeal or 'go begging', as she saw it. However, she did agree to fund-raising events, and the Derby people came to her aid, holding raffles, jumble sales, pub quizzes, and a sponsored walk from Derby to Matlock. It was now thirteen years since the murder, but at last the case came to court.

Roy Brookes told his story again. His stepfather had an obsession with knifes and had boasted that he wanted to kill more women than Jack the Ripper. Roy said he had seen him stab Lynn to death and hide her body in undergrowth near the canal towpath. Michael Brookes opted not to give evidence. The judge, Mr Justice Rougier, gave his verdict immediately. The case was proved, and Flo's family was awarded £10,641 damages. This seemed to Flo a small amount for her granddaughter's death, but in truth the amount was unimportant. In his summary, the judge had stated that Michael Brookes had killed Lynn in a demonic frenzy and that Roy had taken part under duress.

The successful civil case did force the hand of the police, but it was 1992 – fourteen years after the murder – when the police eventually arrested Michael Brookes, charging him with murder. It was a further four years before the case came to court. Roy Brookes was the main witness for the prosecution, and Michael Brookes opted not to speak in his own defence. After a 34-day trial, the jury took nine hours to reach their verdict, and when it came it was one of guilty. Michael Brookes was sentenced to life imprisonment.

Although nothing could bring back Lynn, Flo Siddons now knew that her eighteen-year struggle had come to an end. Her determination to see justice done, and her courage and commitment, make Flo Siddons one of my Derbyshire heroes.

———◆———

11

George Lowe

- member of the 1953 expedition to Mount Everest

Another mountaineer who made Derbyshire his home is George Lowe. He was actually born in New Zealand, and he was a childhood friend of Edmund Hillary. In 1950, George and Edmund went on an expedition to the Himalayas, where they made three journeys to Mount Everest. George Lowe was with Edmund Hillary in his successful 1953 conquest of the world's highest mountain. He recalls that there were nine camps, and at each one there were men servicing the next stage. It was a real team effort, he recalls, and the expedition leader, Sir John Hunt, was a man who appreciated teamwork.

George Lowe set up and remained at the highest camp when Edmund Hilary and Tenzing Norgay made the final assault on the peak and he was there to welcome them back after their success. When Sir Edmund Hilary wrote his book about the conquest of Everest, he dedicated it to 'my old friend George Lowe, for so many years of cheerful comradeship'.

George Lowe had visited Derbyshire to talk to the staff and students of Repton School about the Everest climb, and he came back in 1959 to tell them about his 1958 expedition to the South Pole with Sir Vivian Fuchs. He was also quite keen to find a job. No one on the Everest expedition ever made any money from it. All the photographs, which more mercenary men could have sold for a fortune, were actually given to the Royal Geographical Society. After George's second talk at Repton School, the headmaster, over a glass of sherry, casually asked him what he was going to do next. When George Lowe replied that he wasn't quite sure, he was astounded to be offered a job teaching at Repton. The headmaster told him that he could teach the sixth form boys who were not aiming for university. When asked what he should teach them, the headmaster advised him to 'just make it up as you go along!'

George took the post, and actually sat for his O level in economics with his students. He devised a programme of outdoor activities that included climbing in the Derbyshire peaks. Most of the boys he taught were aiming to go into their fathers' businesses, but they must all look back to their schooldays and think how fortunate they were to have been climbing with one of the heroes of Everest.

12

Bess of Hardwick

*- the second most important woman in
Elizabethan England*

Elizabeth of Hardwick – often known as Bess of Hardwick – left her mark on Derbyshire history and on the Derbyshire landscape. She became one of the most powerful women of her age, second only to her contemporary and namesake Elizabeth I, and she achieved all this by means of her four marriages.

She was born in the old manor house at Hardwick, probably in 1518, though the actual year is disputed. Although her father was the lord of the manor, he was not a wealthy man. The family were 'low level aristocracy', little more than yeoman farmers. Her father died when she was seven, leaving her mother to bring up five children. When Bess was 12, she was sent to live in London to be brought up in the household of Lady Zouch, a distant relation. It was common at the time for children to be educated in manners and household arts in a family other than their own. Families would usually try to place their children in a household of higher status.

In the household of Lady Zouch, young Bess met Robert Barlow, a handsome young man suffering from chronic distemper. Finding that Robert was also from Derbyshire, Bess acted originally through kindness, visiting the delicate young man, and seeing to his diet. Robert soon fell in love with Bess, and, despite his poor health, asked for her hand in marriage. She accepted, and the two families gave their blessing.

Surprisingly, this, the first of Bess's marriages, seems to have been a love match, certainly on his side. Most 16th century marriages were arranged and based on wealth and property, with affection or passion coming in later if the couple were fortunate. However, in the case of Bess and Robert, the hormones kicked in first, the family arrangements following afterwards. It is likely that Bess's mother found Robert suitable because he came of a good Derbyshire family. Perhaps the Barlows thought Bess of Hardwick would be a good person to nurse their sickly son, despite her low dowry. It is probable that at the time of their marriage, both Elizabeth and Robert were well under 16 years of age.

A few months after the wedding, Robert died, and Bess became a widow. She was now wealthy in her own right, as Robert had left her property, including farmland, woodlands, and a number of lead mines. This made Elizabeth quite a catch, but she was in no hurry to remarry. She spent the next fourteen years on her own, running her own affairs and enjoying her independence. Unlike many young women of her age, she was not producing children on an annual basis, and this may have been an element in her good health and future longevity. If she were to marry a second time, her husband would need to be selected with care.

During her late twenties, she was courted by Sir William Cavendish, the Treasurer of the King's Chamber. He was a wealthy widower, with eight children from his first marriage, and was almost twenty years older than Elizabeth. Nevertheless, she accepted him, and they were married at 2 am (!) in August 1547, at the Leicestershire home of William's friend Henry Grey, the Marquis of Dorset.

The marriage was happy, and Elizabeth bore her new husband eight children, six of whom survived. Fortunately

– and this was vital – the surviving six children included three healthy sons. Elizabeth and William chose to live in Derbyshire, possibly because as Protestants they were keeping a low profile during the reign of Catholic Queen Mary. (Mary had, after all, executed their friend Henry Grey and his daughter Jane for plotting to seize her throne for the Protestant cause.)

They lived at Chatsworth Hall, some fifteen miles from Elizabeth's family home at Hardwick. This Chatsworth was not the house of today, but one in a poor state of repair, draughty and uncomfortable. Elizabeth decided that her residence would have to be replaced, and William began to build a fine new home close to the old hall. Wlliam never saw the house completed, however, as he became seriously ill and, despite Elizabeth's nursing, he died in 1557. She was a widow once more, but not for long.

Two years later, Elizabeth married William St Loe, again a widower much older than herself with children of his own. This William was also generous to his wife, and he allowed Elizabeth to continue the work on her Chatsworth home. He also took her to court, and she became one of the ladies of the privy chamber to the new queen, Elizabeth. She renewed her friendship with Catherine Grey, the younger sister of the late Jane. In the highly political atmosphere of the court, this friendship proved dangerous. Catherine was in line to the throne, and when she married without the queen's permission – and even worse became pregnant and gave birth to a son – she and her husband were arrested. Her friend Elizabeth of Hardwick, Lady St Loe, came under suspicion, too, and she was lodged in the Tower of London for a period of seven months. She was determined that on her release she would avoid court intrigue and affairs of state and concentrate on her Derbyshire estates.

Three years later, she found herself a widow for the third time. Despite some stories put about by her late husband's family – poisoning and witchcraft were both mentioned – she inherited his property and wealth. At the age of 44, she was a confident woman with considerable experience and competence in running an estate and managing her own business affairs.

She was also handsome, with red hair and a good complexion. She was still quite a catch, but this time she waited for four years before marrying for the fourth time. She became the wife of George Talbot, the Earl of Shrewsbury, another wealthy widower with property all over the north of England. By now, Elizabeth was well aware of the value of marriage and property. She married her eldest son, Henry, to the earl's eldest daughter, and her youngest daughter, Mary, to the earl's second son. This really was the uniting of two dynasties.

Although Elizabeth's fourth marriage was to last 23 years, it was not a peaceful one. The earl and countess were obliged to have Mary Queen of Scots under their roof as a prisoner-cum-guest, in order to keep her under surveillance for Queen Elizabeth, who was always concerned that her Scottish cousin would lead a Catholic rebellion to seize the English throne. Another of the queen's fears concerned Bess of Hardwick's own granddaughter, Arbella Stuart, another possible contender for the succession to the throne. Bess had to use all her strength of will to prevent her headstrong granddaughter from entering into an unsuitable romantic relationship or, worse still, a betrothal without the queen's prior approval.

The period of marriage to the Earl of Shrewsbury was also one of great trouble for other reasons. Bess and the earl quarrelled frequently, and, towards the end of their marriage, they lived separate lives. He lived at their Chatsworth home, while she lived in her old childhood home at Hardwick, spending a great deal of money in making it much larger and more comfortable. The earl would have liked a legal separation, but the queen insisted that they try to be reconciled. It is possible that the earl found his wife's independence and her Derbyshire spirit hard to bear.

The Earl of Shrewsbury died in 1590, and this time Elizabeth had become a widow in her seventies. She was not interested in yet another marriage, but this determined

Hardwick Hall – 'more glass than wall'. (Julie Saunt)

woman had other projects to pursue. As soon as the earl was dead, Elizabeth set about building a new house at Hardwick, right next to the old manor house. This house, built between 1591 and 1597, was to be a fabulous building summed up soon after its completion in the phrase 'Hardwick Hall, more glass than wall'. It is, perhaps, significant that its six towers bear the initials ES, Elizabeth of Shrewsbury.

Hardwick Hall survives as a splendid example of Elizabethan architecture, little altered since its conception, probably because Bess's descendents preferred to make Chatsworth their home. Bess died in 1608, at the grand old age of 90, an incredible age for that period. During her life she had married and become a widow four times. Each marriage left her more wealthy and more influential. She had enriched the Derbyshire landscape with grand houses at Chatsworth and Hardwick, and in her day she was said to be the second most important woman in the country, after the queen. Bess of Hardwick achieved all this in an era when women were little better than chattels, their husbands taking over their property on marriage.

13

Dennis Skinner

- Labour politician labelled 'the beast of Bolsover'

It might seem unusual to find within a book on Derbyshire heroes the name of a Derbyshire politician, especially when the tabloid newspapers have nicknamed him 'the beast of Bolsover'. The man in question is, of course, the Member of Parliament for Bolsover, Dennis Skinner.

Dennis is a hero to many, and, surprisingly, among those who voice their respect for him are people who do not share his socialist principles. While researching in north Derbyshire, I was told on several occasions, 'I've never voted Labour in my life, but I have to admit that Dennis Skinner is an honest politician, and that's a rare creature.' Another non-socialist told me, 'If Dennis says he'll do something, he does it. He never says one thing and does the opposite.'

Dennis was born in Clay Cross in February 1932. He did well at his local primary school, and, at the age of ten, he was awarded a county scholarship, one of only eighteen in the whole of Derbyshire. He attended Tupton Hall Grammar School from 1942 to 1948. He did well in his school certificate, but decided not to stay on at school. At 16, he left the grammar school and went to work down the pit. 'My parents weren't too happy about it, thinking it was a waste of my education,' Dennis told me recently, 'but I was aware that I was in danger of growing away from my mates. They had all gone down the pit at the age of fourteen.'

The first pit where he worked was Parkhouse Colliery, which he describes as a shallow pit and very cold. He explained that the deeper the pit, the warmer the temperature. His employers would have liked him to work towards becoming a manager, but for him, the pull of the National Union of Mineworkers was much stronger. He became the union delegate for his colliery, and found that his education enabled him to successfully negotiate with the management. 'I could think on my feet, and could calculate figures quicker than they could,' he says.

When Parkhouse Colliery closed, he moved to Glapwell, a much larger colliery, and was soon voted in as vice-president of Derbyshire NUM, becoming county president at the age of 33. He undertook many compensation cases on behalf of his members and was considering becoming a full time union official. At this time, he was asked to stand for election as a councillor. 'Labour had lost control of Clay Cross Urban District Council,' he told me, 'and it was important to win it back.' He stood; he was elected; and his party won back the council majority. His political life continued and he became a county councillor in 1966.

The local member of parliament had expressed his intention to step down, and Dennis was asked to consider standing. He had to weigh up this change in his career against the possibility of full-time union work, but was persuaded to stand. He was elected to the House of Commons in 1970 and has been the member for the Bolsover constituency ever since.

Although Dennis Skinner won the election in Bolsover, the Labour government fell at this election; so he found himself as a backbench MP in the opposition. One story Dennis tells is how he thought he had cracked the system. Soon after he arrived at the House of Commons, there was an evening series of votes going up to midnight. A Conservative MP, keen to leave the Commons and be elsewhere, approached Dennis and asked him if he had a pair. Dennis raised his eyebrows, and the man explained that if the two of them formed a pair, they could each go home without affecting the government majority. Without agreeing to pair, Dennis did advise the man that he should go home. The grateful member hurried away, and the government majority fell by one. A second Conservative approached him with the same request, and he too was dispatched to wherever he wanted to be. After a third one went home, Dennis was sure he had managed to find a way to reduce the government's majority and earn his own party's thanks. It did not work out that way. It was Bob Mellish, the chief Labour whip, who called Dennis to see him the next day. It was not to express his gratitude, but to reprimand him for wrecking the system. It was all based on trust, he explained, and young Dennis Skinner was spoiling it. Dennis tells me that he did explain that he hadn't actually agreed to pair, but had simply advised the Tories to go home. The Labour whip was not amused, and Dennis, not for the last time, was in trouble with his party officials.

Pairing – agreeing with a member of another party to absent oneself from a Parliamentary vote – is one of the things he has never done in his 34 years as an MP. He told me that he has three self-imposed rules: firstly, never to go on foreign trips financed by anyone else: 'If a firm or a foreign country is paying for the trip, they are going to want a payback in some way,' he states. His second abiding principle is never to drink in the House of Commons bar. 'I'm not being puritanical,' he says, 'but the place is full of journalists, listening in to conversations. If an MP has a drink and says something indiscreet, then it'll be in the media the next day.' (I also get the impression that Dennis

Dennis Skinner.

Skinner believes that a miner being drunk at work would be sacked; so why should an MP's workplace be any different.) His third principle is to abstain from pairing, since he feels that if he is being paid to be there, he should not be absent.

Dennis has always been fit. As a young man he took part in athletics, cycling, football, road-walking, cricket and tennis. He even took part in marathons. Although he had smoked as a young miner, he gave up over 30 years ago. It was a bit of a shock, therefore, when in 1999 he discovered he had cancer in the form of a tumour in his bladder. This was removed successfully, and he now needs only an annual check-up. Worse was to happen in 2003, though, when he went for a treadmill test. He collapsed, and was found to be suffering from blocked arteries, which led to his needing a heart bypass.

DENNIS SKINNER

He did admit that at first he had a job to raise his arms, saying that shaving was a problem. However, the Derbyshire politician was back at work within eight weeks, keen to get on with the task he was elected to do: representing his Derbyshire constituents. His fitness must be returning, as he tells me that he walked six miles and also climbed up Kinder Scout, Derbyshire's highest peak, to scatter the ashes of his late brother Gordon. Dennis comes from a close Derbyshire family of seven brothers and two sisters. The whole family is deeply committed to socialist politics. Two of his brothers were members of the Clay Cross Council who were fined under Margaret Thatcher for refusing to put up the rents of council tenants.

Today, Dennis is back in his favourite seat in the House of Commons, just below the central gangway, making things difficult for anyone he thinks is being hypocritical or underhand. He was once forced by the Speaker to withdraw a comment about Mrs Thatcher telling a lie. (Under Parliamentary convention, no MP is capable of telling lies!). He withdrew the word liar, but managed to get away with 'wouldn't recognize the truth if it was sprayed on her eyeballs'.

Dennis Skinner is famous for his humorous asides. I will never forget the occasion when a minister rose to speak with one hand tucked into his pocket. From the direction of Dennis's customary seat, and in a Derbyshire accent, the whole house heard a loud query as to whether the minister was 'playing with hisself'. The embarrassed minister was unable to decide whether to quickly withdraw the offending hand, thus provoking the follow up 'I was right!', or to continue his speech with hand in pocket. I don't think he made the mistake again.

Dennis once had to compete for his accustomed familiar location in the House of Commons with David Owen, then leader of the SDP, who started to leave his prayer card to reserve the seat. Dennis tried attending prayers himself to get his own prayer card in place, but David Owen's card was getting there earlier and earlier. When Dennis found out that he wasn't actually putting it there himself, but was – against all the rules – sending a researcher from his office to do so, he was understandably annoyed. However, the authorities soon put a stop to the practice, and Dennis was back in his old place with his comrades Bob Cryer, Dennis Canavan, and Ioan Evans. The enmity between Dennis Skinner and David Owen continued, until, raising a point of order, Dennis referred to his old enemy as 'a pompous sod'. The speaker, Bernard Weatherall, asked him to withdraw the comment. Dennis said that, as he was feeling in a good mood that day, he was prepared to withdraw the word pompous. As that wasn't the word the speaker wanted withdrawn, and Dennis was adamant, he was kicked out of the House for the day!

Despite being 72, Dennis was keen to return to Parliament after his operation, as he says he still has work to do. He was able to use his experience of how things are done to enable a business park built on the site of former Shirebrook Colliery to provide employment for the families of his constituents, many of them former miners. He also suggested that a spur should be built from near junction 29 of the M1, and a business park built at the former Markham pit. 'They all said the idea of a new motorway junction was mad,' he says, 'but the money has been found and junction 29b will be built.' Dennis is pleased that the two colliery sites will provide 7,000 jobs.

While the 'beast of Bolsover' continues to achieve these things for his people, I reckon he will continue as a truthful and brutally honest politician and a legend in his own lifetime.

14

Brian Clough

- manager of Derby County Football Club 1967–1973

When I was planning this book, I would ask people whom they would include among their Derbyshire heroes. It was remarkable how many replied, 'Apart from Brian Clough, you mean?'

This might be seen as surprising, since Brian Clough was not a Derbyshire man, but a native of Middlesbrough. He spent only six years as manager of Derby County, from 1967 to 1973, but he is still remembered as the most charismatic and the most successful manager the Rams ever had. He had the rare talent that comes along just once in a generation of taking a team of good willing players – with no expensive stars – and turning them into a prize winning team.

It was all done by personality and inspiration. Of course he had coaching skills, but many managers have those. What Cloughie added was his own personal magic. As soon as he and his assistant manager, Peter Taylor, arrived at the Baseball Ground and took charge of the team, things began to change. The team began to win. The Rams had been stuck in the old second division for years, and, to most outside observers, Derby was an average second division team.

Under Brian Clough, the team gained immediate promotion to the first division (the equivalent of today's premier league) and, once there, began to beat teams containing footballers who were household names. They

Brian Clough (Derby Telegraph)

even qualified to play in the European Cup, reaching the semi-final stage in 1972. Very few managers have had that ability to get more out of a team than they knew they had. The only present-day manager with that same inspirational quality is Martin O'Neil, formerly of Leicester City and now of Glasgow Celtic. They appear to posses a magical quality that enables good but not spectacular players to take on and beat the top clubs.

So, what were the qualities that Brian possessed? Well, one was that he ran the team with no interference from the club's directors or from temperamental players. At a later stage in his career, Brian Clough bought the first million pound player. In a TV interview, the player was asked if he were looking forward to playing for his new club on the following Saturday. Clough interrupted to say that *he* selected the team and he would decide whether or not the man was playing! The team had to learn to play his way, and they soon found that it was a winning way.

On the subject of club directors, Cloughie commented, 'There's a seven-man board at Derby and I wouldn't give you tuppence for five of them!' Obviously, this led to resentment on the part of the board, but, while Derby were doing so well on the field and Brian Clough was regarded as a deity by the fans, the board were unable to do much about it. Many of them were well-known Conservative businessmen, who were not happy when Brian Clough went canvassing for their Labour opponents during both general and local elections. Their annoyance was stored up for later use.

Of course, Brian's personality could come over as arrogant to those he criticized, but he could also show amazing and spontaneous generosity to people. His presence lit up the city of Derby, and to the man in the street he could do no wrong, even if some of the more influential citizens found him an irritant.

Brian often appeared on television, where his outspoken views and his willingness to air them made him a popular figure. In October 1973, just after a win against Manchester United, the Derby County board decided to assert their right to run the club their way. Brian Clough and Peter Taylor were sent an ultimatum that instructed them to clear any newspaper articles and television comments with the chairman of the board. Knowing how Brian and Peter would react, this was in fact tantamount to forcing the pair to resign. The manager and assistant did just that; asking the chairman of directors, Sam Longson, for a special meeting of the board at which they could tender their resignations. Their request was refused, and Brian Clough and Peter Taylor were told to send their resignations by post. They did so.

The fans and the players were outraged. At the next match, a home game against Leicester City, Brian Clough sat in the stands and received a standing ovation from the 32,000 spectators. The directors in their box could only watch and seeth. As far as the players were concerned, their loyalty was to Brian Clough. Seven days after his resignation, the directors were handed a letter signed by all the first team squad (except one who was away on business). The letter said that the players were unanimous in their support of Clough and Taylor and asked the board to reinstate them. A copy of the letter was shown to Clough and Taylor, who were visibly moved by what the players had done. Brian, the manager who had always run his team with a rod of iron, was liked and respected by them all. The players even discussed flying to Spain on the following Saturday rather than turning out for Derby County.

However, the Professional Footballers' Association warned the team that they would be in breach of contract. A new manager was appointed and Derby dropped down the table, the dispirited team failing to win their next six games.

When his opponents finally forced him out, Brian Clough committed what many might consider the cardinal sin of becoming the manager of Derby's local arch-rivals, Nottingham Forest, just 15 miles along the A52. Even when he recreated the same miracles at Forest, leading them to dizzy heights, the people of Derby forgave him and looked back on his time at Derby as a special period. Brian continued to live in Derbyshire during his Forest days and he still does. Derby and Brian Clough have a very special relationship.

Derby people often ask why England's greatest club manager never became the manager of the England team. I am sure the reason lies in his outspoken attitude and forceful personality. He would have taken no prisoners, and would not have kowtowed to the England board. Also, it may be that some of the more precious and self-important players would not have appreciated his style.

It is well known that in later years Brian had a problem with alcohol, leading to the need for a liver transplant. He now never drinks, and, unlike certain other ex-footballers, it is certain that he will not lapse. His determination and grit mean that, having decided to give up alcohol, that's what he will stick to.

In Derby, the name of Brian Clough has legendary status. That is why, when asked to name their local heroes, many start their list with his name.

15

Joseph Paxton

- head gardener at Chatsworth House

On 9th May 1826, at 4.30 in the morning, a young man climbed over the back gate of Chatsworth Park, and looked around him. This was no trespasser, however, no would-be burglar intending to rob Chatsworth House. The man was 23 year old Joseph Paxton, the newly appointed head gardener. He had arrived by stagecoach in Chesterfield at 1 am and then walked the 12 miles across the moors to Chatsworth. Finding the main gates locked and no one about to let him in, he had located and climbed the gates by the greenhouses.

By nine o'clock that morning, Joseph had met his under-gardeners and set them to work, and had then taken a cup of tea with the housekeeper Hannah Gregory. He had also met and fallen in love with Mrs Gregory's 26 year old niece, Sarah Bown, a girl he was to marry ten months later. It was not a bad start to his first day.

Joseph had met George Spencer Cavendish, the sixth Duke of Devonshire, while he was working in an arboretum in Chiswick, close by one of the duke's London houses. Speaking to the self-educated young gardener, the bachelor duke was impressed by his knowledge, his intelligence, and his views on what the art of gardening could become. The 36 year old duke was himself a man of vision, with a liberal and progressive outlook, very different from his reactionary father. After this one meeting, the duke decided to employ Joseph Paxton to take charge of the gardens at Chatsworth, which were suffering from 50 years of neglect.

With the duke's encouragement, Joseph went on to transform the gardens at Chatsworth. He constructed a rockery with slabs of stone from the surrounding moors. He built enormous gravity-fed fountains; one of them – the Emperor fountain – was twice as high as Nelson's column. He built a model village, a 300 foot conservatory, and an arboretum. To house the duke's collection of orchids, he built a glasshouse that was 97 feet long, made of wood, and supported by only 16 slender cast-iron columns.

In the five years between 1830 and 1835, Paxton spent the enormous sum of £3,500 just on building glasshouses. Whenever the Duke of Devonshire returned to his Derbyshire home after political duties in London or from diplomatic work abroad, he was always delighted with what Joseph had created at Chatsworth.

Still in his twenties, Paxton launched a new magazine, *The Horticultural Register*. This brought him into conflict with John Claudius Loudon, the editor of the longer established *Gardener's Magazine*. In his magazine, Loudon attacked Paxton over the younger man's preference for wood over metal in the construction of his glasshouses, and Joseph Paxton defended himself in the pages of *The Horticultural Register*.

In a race with Kew Gardens, Joseph succeeded in producing a giant water lily from a cutting found in Guyana. He dedicated this new plant to the queen, whom he had seen visiting Chatsworth as a girl. He named the lily 'Victoria Regis'. As an experiment, he tested its strength by standing his young daughter Annie on one leaf; it bore her weight without difficulty! As the plant needed a heated house – and a huge one at that – Paxton designed a new

Joseph Paxton. (Julie Saunt)

£800 glasshouse, 60 feet by 47 feet. Taking his inspiration from the lily – Paxton considered the plant 'a natural feat of engineering' – he imitated the radiating ribs on the underside of the leaf in the construction of the roof of the lily house.

Through their mutual passion for plants and gardens, the duke and his gardener became friends rather than mere employer and employee. The duke would take Paxton off to Yorkshire to shoot, and the two men would from time to time tour the gardens of other great country houses together, visiting Buckinghamshire, Althorp, and Windsor. In later years the two men would tour Europe together, and their friendship was to last a lifetime.

In 1850, Joseph won a royal commission to design an exhibition building for Prince Albert, after submitting a plan based on the lily house at Chatworth, though on a much vaster scale. The press was very sceptical about his design, claiming that the roof would let in the rain, that the sun coming through all the glass would roast both the exhibits and the exhibitors, and that the atmosphere inside would be so humid that people would be 'drowned in the condensed vapour of their own breath'. However, based on his experience of building glasshouses at Chatsworth, Paxton was very confident in his design.

The building – known as the Crystal Palace – took 2,000 men only eight months to build at a cost of less than £80,000. Its construction required 60,000 cubic feet of wood, and 4,500 tons of iron. When it was built, the Crystal Palace with its 293,000 panes of glass was breathtaking. It was 1,848 feet in length, 408 feet wide, and 108 feet in height. It was on such a grand scale that Queen Victoria and Prince Albert were able to drive through it in their carriage. The critics changed their tune, and the newspapers now hailed the building as 'a palace of glass', 'a hall of light', and 'a temple of enchantment'.

In later years, Joseph Paxton's activities took him away from Chatsworth. He founded a newspaper, *The Daily News*, appointing Charles Dickens as its editor. He accompanied the duke on a voyage round the world. Joseph even went on, with the duke's encouragement, to become the Liberal MP for Coventry, but he never forgot his spiritual home in Derbyshire.

On his death, in June 1865, at the age of 61, Joseph Paxton's body was taken back to Chatsworth. He was buried alongside the sixth duke, who had died seven years earlier. It seems fitting that the two friends and fellow plant-enthusiasts, one born an aristocrat and the other born into poverty, now lie side by side in Edensor churchyard.

16

Ellen MacArthur

- the sailor from Whatstandwell

Few people will be amazed to find Derbyshire heroes who are climbers and speleologists, since the county is famous for its peaks and caves. However, to find that this country's most famous young female sailor hails from Derbyshire is more surprising. Yet, Ellen MacArthur was born on a smallholding in Whatstandwell in rural Derbyshire, 80 miles from the sea. Her parents were both teachers, though her mother gave up for a while to bring up the children. Her father was a teacher of technology and craft design, and an avid collector of tools and old machinery.

As a child, she was sent to ballet lessons but didn't enjoy them; so – at the age of four – she rebelled and refused to go any more. She had much more fun playing cricket, helping her stonemason grandfather, and climbing in the hay barn. From the beginning, Ellen was a real tomboy.

Her contact with sailing and the sea came from visiting the east coast to see her Auntie Thea, who owned a small boat called *Cabaret*. After just one holiday on *Cabaret*, Ellen was smitten. She spent hours looking through boat magazines, and, like me, she read all Arthur Ransom's books: *Swallows and Amazons*, *Coot Club*, *We Didn't Mean To Go To Sea*, etc. She dreamt of owning her own boat, and saved all her pocket money in a box she kept on the radiator in her bedroom, putting a tick on a square of graph paper every time she had another pound. And, every year, there was the annual holiday on Thea's boat to look forward to. *Cabaret* was not a large boat. It was 20 feet in length, and built for four; so, with seven people and a dog on board, holidays were a bit of a tight squeeze!

The first holidays were spent exploring rivers and sailing down the east coast, but later ones involved crossing the North Sea to Belgium and Holland. Even when it was stormy, Ellen never felt afraid. One of her favourite memories was in the port of Dunkirk, when she was allowed to take the boat's dinghy and go off by herself.

By the time Ellen was nine, she had saved £200, and, with a generous donation from her grandmother, she managed to buy a fibreglass six-foot dinghy, which she named *Threep'ny Bit*. When her bedroom proved too small to house all her sailing equipment, she simply moved her bed into the barn, where she slept in a sleeping bag. The boat she kept on a nearby trout pond, where she spent all her time dreaming of adventures.

Some of her earliest sailing had been on Ogston Reservoir, near Matlock, but, at the age of 16, she went on a number of courses run by the David King Nautical School in Hull. After her first week's training, David commented to her parents, 'I don't know where your daughter's going, but wherever it is, she'll go a long way on water.' In fact, Ellen did so well that she was allowed to skip the two intermediate courses – 'Competent Crew' and 'Coastal Skipper' – and to take the advanced course, called 'Yachtmaster', which involved clocking up 2,500 miles at sea.

She had been aiming for a career as a veterinary surgeon, but just before her A levels, she contracted glandular fever, which involved time off school. At home recuperating, she watched on TV the Whitbread race, a competition for high-tech 60-foot yachts. Although the idea of crewed sailing didn't appeal, it did make up Ellen's mind that her future lay at sea rather than as a vet.

Threep'ny Bit had been replaced by *Kestrel*, which was now traded in for *Iduna*, a 21 foot Corribee, which Ellen describes as 'a tough little lady . . . a real little sea boat'. Ellen had to use all her Derbyshire grit and hard bargaining skills to persuade the owner of *Iduna* to do a direct swap for *Kestrel,* with no cash involved. She got her way and says, 'He even threw in an engine and a jib.' She also adds that her boyfriend of the time was a bit shocked to discover just how single-minded she could be when a boat was involved.

By now, she was spending a lot of time sailing at Hull, and was thrilled to be asked to crew on a racing yacht called *Panic Major*. This vessel had taken part in a French non-stop single-handed round the world race called the Vendée Globe. Weekends on the *Panic Major* turned into whole weeks, and Ellen became a regular crewmember. She learned everything she could about sailing a racing yacht and how to make repairs at sea. Nevertheless, she was startled when one day, after the crew had disembarked, the owner announced that he was going for a sleep and Ellen could take it the 60 miles from Bridlington to Hull without his help. She managed it, and it was a day of great pride and exhilaration for her.

She was amazed to find out that David King had entered her for the title of the British Telecom/Yachting Journalists' Association Young Sailor of the Year. She was more than amazed to win the title and to be invited to a presentation in London, where she was photographed with one of her heroes, Robin Knox-Johnston, the first man to sail round the world single-handed.

Still only 18, Ellen became an instructor at the nautical

Ellen MacArthur (Derby Telegraph)

school in Hull, often teaching people many times her own age. She also decided that she was going to use *Iduna* to sail single-handed round the coast of Great Britain. She planned to sail anti-clockwise, going north from Hull along the east coast of Scotland. The prospect of storms forced Ellen to take *Iduna* through the Caledonian Canal, rather than round the north of Scotland. She then sailed south, with stopovers in Fishguard and Solva, Southampton and Chichester, before sailing up through the North Sea back to Hull. The journey took four and a half months, and Ellen says that she grew up on the trip. During it, she had made decisions for and by herself. Facing storms, the stress of feeling unwell, taking on the sole responsibility for herself and her boat,

ELLEN MACARTHUR

she learned how to stay calm and make decisions in every different situation. She had learned self-reliance.

Ellen's MacArthur's self confidence and the intensity of her passion for sailing were often tested. At one time, she found herself desperately seeking sponsors, while living in a portacabin and spending only £10 a week on her food. It must have brought back memories of her schooldays, when she would frequently save her dinner money in order to put it towards buying a boat.

Ellen spent the next few years preparing herself for the world's toughest race: the Vendée Globe. Her preparations included competing in – and winning – a two-handed race round the UK and Ireland, followed by the Mini Transat (as its name suggests, a transatlantic crossing for small yachts), and then the 4,000 mile Route de Rhum. The latter is a single-handed race from St Malo in France to Guadeloupe in the Caribbean. Ellen undertook this three-week race in *Kingfisher*, a chartered 50-foot boat, named after her new sponsors, the Kingfisher Group. Despite problems with the staysail and with a burst hydraulic pipe in the motor which controlled the keel, Ellen won her class in the Route de Rhum and even beat eight of the twelve boats in the 60-foot class.

Ellen was touched to be awarded the *Jeune Espoire de Voile* award (which translates as 'young hope of sailing'), especially as she was the first non-French person to get it. The French take their sailing very seriously, and 22 year old 'petite Ellen' had become one of their favourite heroines.

At this point, she began to think seriously about the Vendée Globe, hoping that the Kingfisher group would sponsor her again. She understood their concerns about sending out a young woman in her early twenties and only 5 feet 2 inches tall, in a single-handed race that would circumnavigate the world and that would last for three, four, or even five months. Fortunately, she was able to convince them that, in spite of her youth and stature, she was capable of competing with the best single-handed sailors in the world.

The new *Kingfisher*, a 60-foot boat, was built in New Zealand. Ellen sailed it back the 12,000 miles to the UK with three friends. It must have caused some inconvenience, because, although it had all the latest technical equipment built in, it had neither a toilet nor a shower. In June 2000, Ellen competed in the Europe New Man Singlehanded TransAtlantic Race from Plymouth to Newport in the USA. When she won it, she became, at 23, the youngest winner since the race's inception in 1960.

Ellen was now ready to undertake the Vendée Globe, the race she had always dreamt of tackling. Before she did, she returned to Derbyshire, where her Uncle Glynn, a GP, helped her check the medical box she would be taking on the race. Its contents were startling and included pre-threaded needles for sewing up open wounds, pain killers, drugs for serious infections, and a kit for setting broken bones. Ellen was very conscious of what it would mean to be on her own for months at sea: every accident would entail her being her own doctor and surgeon.

Back in France, in Les Sables d'Orlonne, Ellen found that excitement was mounting as the race got nearer. There were huge crowds and the young Derbyshire woman was always being asked for her autograph. There were 24 of the world's most high-tech racing boats competing, crewed by 24 of the world's most experienced sailor-adventurers. Most of the boats were 60-footers, though there were some 50-foot vessels, unlikely to win but just wanting to compete in the race. Ellen was one of only two women in the race, and one of four Brits.

ELLEN MACARTHUR

The race got underway on 5th November, and cheering crowds chanting Ellen's name lined the banks. These would be the last people she would see for the next hundred days. One of the most difficult problems on a single-handed voyage is that of sleep. Ellen had trained herself to take short catnaps, and throughout the whole journey she slept in 12-minute bursts, before waking to check the instruments, the weather, her position, and the condition of the boat.

Her route led her south and then east round the tip of Africa. It continued east, sailing south of both Australia and New Zealand, and then across the southern Pacific to Cape Horn, before heading north-east across the Atlantic. At times she was so far south that she was nearer to Antarctica than to Australia. Throughout her journey, she recorded her feelings and experiences to the onboard cameras, as well as in her emails home. The sheer exhilaration of surfing through the Southern Ocean at 45 knots and delight in seeing whales and albatrosses were contrasted by low times when tactics went wrong or equipment broke down. No one who has seen the footage will ever forget the sight of Ellen's intense emotion and exhaustion after she had spent two hours up the mast fighting the most horrendous conditions to repair a broken batten.

As she sailed north through the Atlantic, it appeared for a while as if Ellen might actually win the race, but a broken forestay put paid to that. Eventually she sailed into Les Sables harbour, 94 days after leaving it. Only one boat, that of Frenchman Michael Desjoyeaux, had returned ahead of her; thirteen others were to come in days, weeks, and even months later; a further nine had been forced to retire.

Ellen MacArthur came second in the world's most prestigious single-handed race, and she became the youngest Briton ever to circumnavigate the globe and the fastest woman to have done so. She was awarded an MBE and won the Helen Rollason award for courage and achievement in the face of adversity. The French press dubbed Ellen the greatest Englishwoman since Jane Austen – not bad for a girl from a landlocked English county.

Ellen has always been a strong family person. She is close to her parents, who, she says, come to see her off on her journeys looking both proud and concerned. She grew up with both her maternal grandmother and her paternal grandparents living close by. The whole extended family lived within walking distance, and this must have given Ellen the strong family foundation that enabled her to go out and become an international adventurer.

One of Ellen's own heroes is Irene Lewis, her mother's mother, who gained a degree from Derbyshire University at the age of 83, just a few months before her death. She must have shared with Ellen that Derbyshire grit and determination.

———◆———

17

Catherine Booth

- 'mother' of the Salvation Army

Catherine Mumford was born in the town of Ashbourne on 17th January 1829, but it is under her married name – Catherine Booth – that she became well known. With her husband, William, Catherine founded the Salvation Army, and she was dubbed 'the mother of the Army'.

Her mother, Sarah, had been brought up in the Church of England, but converted to Methodism as a young woman. She began to dress plainly, wore her hair in a simple style, and gave up worldly activities such as playing cards, dancing, and going to the theatre. She met and fell in love with a travelling Methodist lay preacher named John Mumford when he came to Ashbourne. He was a carriage-builder by trade, and was committed to total abstinence from drink, though in later life he gave up both religion and abstinence.

John and Sarah married and had four sons – three of whom died – and one daughter, Catherine, known as Kate. Kate and her brother were brought up in a very strict household. Sarah was concerned that meeting other children might corrupt them. She also worried that teachers might encourage false values and poor morals, and pronounced that public education would endanger her children's souls. Given her beliefs on this subject, it is surprising that she did eventually allow Kate to go to school from the age of twelve to fourteen, presumably after checking the teachers' views and ideals and finding that they coincided with her own. Kate studied English composition, mathematics, history, and geography, and her horizons were expanded by this contact with education and with people outside her own family.

At the age of 14, Kate Mumford developed a problem with her spine, which confined her to bed, and so her education was once more under the strict supervision of her mother. Now she studied only theology and church history. The reading of fiction was banned as a frivolous activity, as was anything to do with France and the French language. It is difficult to decide whether this Francophobia was of religious origin or simply parochialism. Kate Mumford was kept from meeting others, so that her only friend was her brother, John, and she must have felt even more isolated after he emigrated to America at the age of sixteen. Kate's severe and confining childhood does not appear to have made her resentful or rebellious, however, because she was to rear her own children in exactly the same manner.

In 1852, Catherine Mumford and her mother heard a young Wesleyan preacher named William Booth. William, from Nottingham, was 23 years of age, the same age as Kate. After the meeting, a debate followed concerning the virtue of abstinence compared with the 'vice' of mere temperance. The most ardent speaker for total abstinence was Catherine Mumford, and William Booth was later to recall that 'on that day I fell head over heels in love with the woman who would one day become my wife'.

One of the few subjects upon which Catherine and William ever disagreed was whether women were suitable to preach. Catherine believed that 'in Christ there is no male or female' and that all who are called should be able to proclaim the Word. William's original view was that women were not mentally as capable as men, but he did have to admit he was wrong on this topic. In later life he would be very glad that he had given way.

William was considering becoming a preacher in the Congregationalist church, but Catherine had problems with the Calvinist concept that the elect who would inherit eternal life were preordained. She believed that people could effect their salvation through their beliefs and behaviour throughout their life, that it wasn't preordained. Again, William came to accept Catherine's opinion.

William Booth and Catherine Mumford were married in 1855, and their life together was to last for another 35 years. They became a united and mutually supporting team. They had eight children and brought them up as vegetarians. Catherine had a great deal of concern for animals and their welfare and was a lifelong opponent of fox hunting, considering it barbaric. Unlike the conventional Christian view that animals could have no life after death because they had no souls, Catherine believed that there might be the possibility of an afterlife for them.

Although she always took a full part in the work of her church, Catherine was very much opposed to holding bazaars to raise funds, seeing them as worldly, especially if lotteries were involved. Like her mother before her, she dressed her family very simply and plainly. On one occasion, she wrote to thank her mother for a dress sent to one of the children but then went on to criticize the frock for being too pretty!

William became an itinerant evangelical preacher for the New Connexion denomination, and the couple led a nomadic existence. He preached to many revival meetings, but did arouse some resentment and jealousy among his fellow ministers because of the size of his congregations –

2,000 at some meetings. He was forced to settle down, first at Brighouse and then Gateshead. In Brighouse, Catherine taught a class of women members and ran a Sunday school for girls. In Gateshead, she would lead prayers and she began to call at the houses of women in working class areas, persuading them to come to meetings. She also tried to persuade their husbands to sign the pledge to give up alcohol. In one period of two weeks, she got ten men to sign!

William and Catherine began to hold street processions, singing hymns to encourage the crowds to join them. At times, their singing had to compete with drunks coming out of the pubs to mock them. When William had a nervous breakdown, Catherine took over many of his duties until he was well again. William always longed to get back to being a travelling evangelist but was thwarted by his enemies and rivals. Eventually, in 1861, he left the Connexion movement, to go 'freelance'.

The year 1865 found William and Catherine in London; he was in the East End, preaching to the poor, and she was in the West End, preaching to the better off. At this time, Catherine was certainly the better-known preacher, and she provided almost all the family income. A woman preacher was still a novelty, however. A poster for one of her meetings read 'Come and hear a woman preach!' The East End Christian Mission expanded throughout the country, and the East End part of its title was dropped.

Although the Booths had broken away from the New Connexion movement because of the autocratic attitude of some of its leaders, they did have some of that quality themselves. They were most put out when some of their missions, like the one in Leicester, broke away to become independent. Eventually, William decided that God's work would be better served by a military hierarchy than by a committee-based democracy.

The Salvation Army was born in 1878. While holding to the tenets of the Christian Mission, it used military ranks, and there was a uniform. Converts became soldiers; class leaders were known as sergeants; evangelists became captains and lieutenants, and William Booth became the general.

While the change from Mission to Army was William's idea, Catherine had a great deal of input into its doctrines and methods. She designed the uniform that the women soldiers and officers would wear, including those memorable bonnets, making sure that it should be plain, simple and modest. Although women had equal status in the Salvation Army and were encouraged to become captains and lieutenants, Catherine Booth herself was never given a rank. She was content to be known as the mother of the Army. She was delighted that her daughters and her sons all joined the Salvation Army. In fact, one of her daughters, Evangeline, was to become the first woman general of the Salvation Army, holding that post from 1934 to 1939.

Many onlookers were scandalized to see young Salvation Army women – known as hallelujah lasses – march through the streets behind brass bands, preaching in the open air and in churches. It was thought vulgar when the Salvation Army began so sing religious words to well-known pub tunes, on the grounds of 'why should the devil have all the best tunes?' Although many were shocked by these antics, the Army began to attract girls from all backgrounds. Working class girls joined, but also girls from more privileged families, the daughters of doctors and clergymen. The Salvation Army was the one place where they could play a full and equal role. As early as 1880, 46 of the 138 missions, now known as corps, had women officers in charge.

The Salvation Army quickly spread throughout the country, and then to the USA, Canada, Australia, Europe, and even India. Today it is present in 109 countries. It is undoubtedly true to say that, without the influence of Catherine Booth, the Salvation Army would have taken a very different form. The Salvation Army men and women are a familiar sight on the streets of every town and city, selling *The War Cry*. They are a supporter of the Fairtrade Foundation, and they continue to preach abstinence from alcohol. It should be noted that one of Catherine Booth's

Ashbourne Park's statue of Catherine. (David Moorley)

converts was her father. She was overjoyed to be able to rescue him from his alcoholism, and bring him back 'into the fold'. It was not only drinkers who were saved. Fallen women were targeted and persuaded to become 'born again'. Catherine was shocked at just how young some of these prostitutes were, and she was very active in the successful campaign to raise the age of consent in girls from twelve to sixteen.

Catherine continued to preach right up until her death in October 1890. One man, not a member of the organization, was so impressed when he heard her that he commented that, if he were ever charged with a crime, he would not want to be represented in court by any of the top lawyers; he would want Catherine Booth! She is remembered all over the world and particularly in her native town of Ashbourne, where her statue graces the local memorial gardens. Interestingly, the statue has been positioned so that it faces Catherine's childhood home, a cottage in Sturston Road.

———◆———

18

Joe Payne

- the stuff of football legends

Another of Derbyshire's sporting heroes was footballer Joe Payne, born at Brimmington Common in 1914. Joe played at centre forward for his local team, Bolsover Colliery. He was spotted by a talent scout from Luton Town, and Luton signed him. However, Joe was never used as a centre forward but spent his first two years there as a reserve half back.

Then, on Easter Monday 1936, a big match was coming up. Luton were lying second in the league, and were due to play Bristol Rovers. It was vital that they win, but their centre forward was injured, and both replacement strikers were on the sick list. Luton had no manager at the time, and the team was being picked by a selection committee. As they pondered the difficult situation, having no striker for such an important match, there seemed no solution.

Luckily, someone remembered that young Joe Payne had played at centre forward for his Derbyshire colliery team before being signed by Luton. In desperation, Joe was given the number nine shirt with the advice to 'just go out and do your best'. It was clear that the committee were not expecting much from him.

For Joe Payne, it was a real Roy-of-the-Rovers situation, and what followed was incredible. 'Just do your best', he'd been told, and Joe's *best* that day included scoring ten of Luton's twelve goals. That record – ten goals in a match – has never been beaten. In fact, the nearest ever reached was

JOE PAYNE

'Ten-goal Payne'.

seven goals by one player, which puts Joe's fantastic achievement into perspective.

Joe always deflected the fame and glory heaped on him by the local and national press that day by saying that the players who had set up the goals were as important as the man who had put them into the net. Joe – now, of course, nicknamed Ten-Goal Payne – kept his centre forward position and scored 55 goals in the following season, enabling Luton to gain promotion.

After winning a national cap by playing for England in a match against Finland in May 1937, Joe went on to play for Chelsea. When ankle injuries caused him to give up football, he concentrated on cricket. Again, he achieved a high standard, playing at county level.

But Joe's hero status is not due to his county cricket or even his inclusion in a national soccer team. His fame is due to the day in 1936 when he was thrown in as a last-minute choice for his club and became a legend.

19

Joseph Wright

- 18th-century painter

Many well-known artists were born in Derbyshire, and many others have come to this beautiful county to paint, but the artist most closely associated with it was Joseph Wright. Historians and art critics always refer him as Wright of Derby, thus planting him firmly in this location.

He was born at 28 Irongate in Derby in 1734, the son of a lawyer, who also acted as Derby's town clerk. Joseph had two elder brothers, who became a lawyer and a doctor, respectively. After an education at Derby Grammar School, Wright trained for two years in London under the artist Thomas Hudson, a leading portrait painter. On his return to Derby, he painted a self-portrait and several portraits of his family and friends. He was not satisfied with these early attempts, and in 1756 he returned to the studio of Thomas Hudson for a further fifteen months' study. He then set up a portrait painting practice, with clients in Derby, Lincoln, Newark, and other Midland towns and cities.

He became a wonderful portraitist, capturing the personality of his subjects, as well as painting a true likeness. He painted all the great and good of his day, including Sir Richard Arkwright and his family and Jedediah Strutt, Arkwright's partner. Sometimes his honest pictures did not please his sitters, as he painted in all their physical attributes, good and bad. Not everyone wanted a warts-and-all portrait of the kind Oliver Cromwell had demanded of his painter. Ladies were perturbed to see their double chins shown in their portraits, and men their ample paunches. His picture of Sarah Carver and her daughter are a clear example of his naturalism! However, viewed today, these honest pictures do capture the people in them; the realism of the likenesses give us more pleasure than the more flattering paintings of less truthful artists.

Nevertheless, his honesty may have led some potential sitters to avoid him. Fortunately, Joseph Wright was much more than a painter of portraits. He became widely known for his candlelight paintings, in which the subjects are illuminated by the light of candles and lamps. The drama of these pictures is heightened by the strong contrast of darkness and light. Artists like Caravaggio had done this much earlier, but it was almost unknown among English painters.

Early self-portrait of Wright of Derby.
(By kind permission of Derby Museum and Art Gallery)

JOSEPH WRIGHT

Paintings in this style include subjects as varied as the death scene in Romeo and Juliet, a blacksmith working in his forge, a Lake District scene of a waterfall, and a rainbow at a location near Chesterfield. Wright's landscape pictures are reminiscent of both Turner and Constable, though of course Wright predates those two painters by a generation.

In 1774–5, he toured Italy and while there he saw Mount Vesuvius erupt. This inspired many dramatic paintings of the volcano, using darkness and fire. He also painted Italian scenes of grottos by moonlight, and night scenes lit by fireworks. Sources of light, and their effect, continued to fascinate the Derby painter.

Where Joseph Wright was a genuine original, however, was in the paintings he did of scientific subjects. He had many friends in the Lunar Society, the Midlands-based group of enlightened scientists and progressive thinkers. He knew, and painted, Erasmus Darwin, the scientist cum poet cum inventor (and the grandfather of Charles Darwin). Other friends included the Derby clockmaker and geologist John Whitehurst, as well as Josiah Wedgewood, James Watt, and Matthew Boulton and it was his contact with these men that led him to paint pictures connected with science.

A Philosopher Lecturing on the Orrery shows a lecturer talking to his students, who include a young woman and children as well as men, and using a model of the planets and an oil lamp to demonstrate an eclipse. The light from the lamp illuminates the faces of the onlookers, and is said to represent the light of scientific knowledge. This painting was exhibited at the Society of Artists in London and was bought for the sum of £210 by the wealthy fifth Earl Ferrers of Staunton Harold on the Derbyshire–Leicestershire border. The Alchymist Discovering Phosphorus is, despite the reference to alchemy, another painting showing a scientific

A Philosopher Lecturing on the Orrey by Joseph Wright.
(By permission of Derby Museum and Art Gallery)

experiment, again lit to tremendous effect. Both paintings can now be seen, with more than 20 other Wright paintings at Derby Art Gallery. A third painting relating to science is *An Experiment on a Bird in an Air Pump*, which is displayed at the National Gallery in Trafalgar Square.

It was not just local patrons like Earl Ferrers who patronized Wright. Catherine the Great of Russia and Lord Palmerston both bought Wright's work during his lifetime. In 1768, he was described by a reviewer in *The Gazette* as 'a great and uncommon genius'.

Joseph Wright married Hannah Swift in 1773, and they had six children, though three of them died in childhood. Some members of Derby society considered that Joseph had 'married beneath him', but Joseph and Hannah married for love, not for the purpose of social standing. Love matches were not so common in 1773. Joseph Wright took part in Derby life, and, as a talented flute player, he frequently went to musical evenings held at the home of one of his friends, who was the organist at All Saints' church.

Joseph died at the age of 63 in his Derby home, having continued to paint right up to his death in August 1797. He was buried in the churchyard of St Alkmund, but, following the demolition of that church in 1967, his tombstone was moved to St Werburgh's churchyard in Cheapside.

In 2003, one of Joseph Wright's paintings – a portrait of Richard Arkwright junior, his wife, Mary, and his daughter Anne – was due to be sold to an American buyer by its private owner. Given the Derbyshire connection of both the painter and the Arkwright family, local art lovers and the Arkwright Society were among those who were determined that the picture should remain in Britain – and, ideally, should come to Derbyshire. A group called the Derwent Valley Mills Partnership launched a campaign and eventually £1.2 million pounds was raised and the picture was bought. It has now joined the Wright collection in Derby Art Gallery. Another campaign has since been launched to prevent the sale to America of two further Wright paintings: one of Sir Richard Arkwright's cotton mills in Cromford, and the other of his home, Willersley Castle.

20

Phoebe Brown

- Derbyshire's strongest woman

Phoebe Brown lived in Matlock in the first half of the 19th century and was famous as Derbyshire's strongest woman. She became one of the local tourist attractions; visitors would come to Matlock not only to see the imposing Heights of Abraham and the beautiful River Gardens, but also to stare at the woman they called the Amazon of Matlock Green!

She was a blacksmith, a carpenter, and a stonemason. She was an expert on horses, and her opinion on the worth of a horse was always sought after. It was said that Phoebe could ride as well as any jockey from Newmarket. She was a crack shot with a gun, as well as a noted pugilist, who could fight in the boxing ring as well as her male counterparts.

A contemporary local historian wrote, 'Her step is more manly than any man's and can cover 40 miles a day. She undertakes any kind of manual labour, as holding the plough, driving the team, thatching the barn, using the flail, but her chief avocation is breaking horses at a guinea a week. Her voice is more than masculine and with the wind in her favour she can send it a mile.'

However, this Amazon also had less physical interests. She loved poetry, and could quote from Shakespeare, Milton, and Alexander Pope. Phoebe was a skilled musician, playing the bass viol, the violin, and the flute. It must have been quite an unusual sight to see this big woman, over six feet tall, with the build of a navvy, playing sensitively on the flute! Her practical skills and her musical talents came together when a wealthy visitor made her a present of a harpsichord. It was too large for Phoebe's house, so she simply set to building a new wing to accommodate the instrument.

Phoebe did like to receive visitors, but one lady who came made the mistake of saying that if Phoebe were ever in Liverpool she should make a return visit. She was somewhat taken aback when some time later Phoebe rode up on horseback, wearing a man's coat and hat, a large petticoat, and several kerchiefs tied around her neck.

Phoebe Brown had a morbid fear of being robbed, and her house became a fortress, containing a veritable arsenal of weapons: swords and daggers, fowling-pieces and muskets, and bayonets and spears, which she had made herself at the forge. Despite her fears, it was always unlikely that any burglar would break into the house. Apart from the weapons she had for self-defence, there was always the chance of being tackled by the lady herself. On one occasion, when Phoebe was walking home in the dark, a man tried to sexually molest her. Whether he was drunk or insane is not recorded, but the would-be Lothario was left lying beaten and bruised at the side of the road.

On the death of Phoebe Brown in 1854, a local clergyman poet wrote an epitaph for her which read:

Here lies romantic Phoebe
Half Gannymede and half Hebe;
A maid of mutable condition,
A jockey, cowherd and musician.

21

Jack Bodell

- British Heavyweight Boxing Champion

The first time many people had heard of the Derbyshire town of Swadlincote was in the early 1970s, when a local man, Jack Bodell, became the British Heavyweight Boxing Champion. The national press were dumbstruck. Before the match, they had given the Derbyshire man no chance against their golden boy, Joe Bugner.

On the night of 27th September 1971, Bugner was cheered as he climbed into the ring at the Empire Pool at Wembley Stadium and Jack Bodell was booed. Jack Bodell was 31, ten years older than Bugner, and the unglamorous Midlander was given no chance against his opponent. The boxing commentators, all based in the south, thought that the stylish Joe Bugner would give the awkward southpaw Jack Bodell a boxing lesson. It was billed as a contest between beauty and the beast.

They all had to eat their words. An hour later, after 15 hard-fought rounds, Jack Bodell, as the undisputed heavyweight champion of Britain, Europe, and the Commonwealth, left the ring to the cheers of his newly converted fans. The unthinkable had happened: the unfashionable beast had trounced the unstoppable beauty.

It was only in Derbyshire that boxing fans were not surprised. They had known about Jack Bodell for years. He was an amiable, good-natured giant.

One other person who was not surprised when Jack Bodell

beat the much younger Bugner was the former champion Henry Cooper, who had fought both men. Before the Wembley contest, Henry had told the *Derby Telegraph*, 'I don't think Bugner will be able to handle Jack. I don't think he has had the experience to cope. He will find that he has never met anyone as awkward or as difficult.' At the time, though, Henry's comments were lost in a chorus of experts who knew better.

One such 'expert', who had written that if Bodell beat Bugner, he would personally go to Swadlincote and clean the Derbyshire boxer's windows, was John Desmond Hacket of the *Daily Express*. A couple of days after the fight, Hacket received a call from Jack Bodell saying that the bucket and wash-leather were waiting, but where was the reporter? To the journalist's credit, he did travel up to

Jack Bodell. (Magic Attic)

Derbyshire and perform the task, watched by Jack in a deckchair and a crowd of Swadlincote folk shouting advice. 'Hey up, Hacket, you've missed a bit!' was the mildest comment. 'Sort the bugger out, Jack,' was more typical. I think the journalist had as much trouble in finding Swadlincote as he did in cleaning the windows in front of a critical crowd of spectators!

So, who was this Derbyshire hero, Jack Bodell? Jack came from a local boxing family. His Uncle Sid was a manager, and his Uncle Tom was himself a notable boxer. Indeed, some Swad folk even claim that Tom Bodell was better than Jack, though that is probably going a little too far. It is said – though it is difficult to say how accurately – that earlier Bodells were bare-fist boxers. It is certainly true that when local fairs came to Swad, the boxing booth proprietors banned the local Bodells from taking part.

The Bodells worked in the mines and so media claims that Jack was a chicken farmer or a swineherd were something of a myth, but, as local people frequently point out, most mining families kept a pig and a few chickens. The tabloids liked the swineherd label because they could coin the alliterative nickname 'Jack the Swadlincote Swineherd'.

Jack Bodell began his boxing career at Coalville Amateur Boxing Club, winning 96 of his 102 bouts and becoming the British amateur cruiserweight champion before turning professional in 1962. In that year he won the Midlands light-heavyweight title, before moving up to heavyweight. He had 49 fights between 1962 and 1966, winning 42 of them and becoming the Midlands heavyweight champion. In June 1967, he moved into a whole new league, fighting the immortal Henry Cooper for the British and Empire title. Although he lost to Cooper, Jack fought and beat every other heavyweight British boxer of the day, often travelling to meet them on their own patch. He beat Johnny Prescott in Wolverhampton, Carl Gizzi in Cardiff, Billy 'golden boy' Walker at Wembley, and rugged Brian London in Liverpool.

When the world champion, Cassius Clay (later renamed Muhammad Ali), had a fight coming up against a difficult southpaw, he asked who was the most awkward boxer of that style. Boxers with an orthodox stance lead with their left hand, saving their right for the big punch, whereas southpaws lead with their right. Although southpaw fighters are used to boxing against orthodox boxers, most orthodox fighters dread coming up against a southpaw. Clay employed Bodell to go over to America to become his sparring partner, so that the world champ could get used to the southpaw style.

In 1969, Henry Cooper relinquished his British and Empire heavyweight title following a dispute with the British Boxing Board, and Jack Bodell beat Carl Gizzi to become the heavyweight champion for the first time. However, the following year 'our 'Enry' came back and regained his title from Jack Bodell, though the Derbyshire man took Cooper the full distance and acquitted himself well. To the amazement of all, Henry Cooper lost his title in March 1971 to a young Joe Bugner, losing by a quarter of a point in a controversial decision.

In the meantime, Jack Bodell fought and beat a number of good opponents, including Manuel Ramos and giant Jack O'Halloran. Then, in September 1971, Jack was back in the ring challenging the new champion, Joe Bugner, for the combined British, European, and Commonwealth heavyweight title. It is always satisfying when the self-appointed experts get it so spectacularly wrong. The boxer from south Derbyshire, the man they dismissed as a clumsy and inelegant country bumpkin and the boxer the London

'Hey up – you missed a bit!' (Magic Attic)

fans loved to boo, was now the undisputed champion of the whole country, as well as the Commonwealth and Europe. Ah, yes!

110

22

Barnes Wallis

- inventor of the bouncing bomb

Barnes Neville Wallis was born in Ripley on 26th September 1887, the second son of a general practitioner in the town. When Barnes was still a boy, his father became ill with poliomyelitis. Although Dr Wallis managed to struggle on as a GP, it was Barnes' mother who had to take on the task of running the family and making ends meet.

When Barnes was 12, his mother urged him to sit a competitive exam for Christ's Hospital school. He passed, and at the school he excelled in English, science, and maths. Barnes never forgot the debt he owed to both his mother and his science teacher. He left school at 17, taking an apprenticeship at a London engineering works and then transferring to J.S. White's shipyard at Cowes.

He did well there, and, after qualifying, he had the good fortune to work alongside H.B. Pratt, an engineer who had worked at Vickers designing rigid airships. Pratt soon noticed and appreciated Barnes Wallis's flair for design and persuaded him to move with him when he returned to Vickers in Barrow. There the two men, together with another engineer called Temple, formed a formidable team of airship engineers.

Wallis served in the Artist's Rifles and the RNVR during the First World War. After the war, Pratt and Temple gave up work on airships, but Barnes Wallis continued to design and build the R80, a streamlined airship universally acclaimed as the best airship of its day. When, following the R38 disaster, the government abandoned its interest in airships, Barnes Wallis went on to study for a degree in engineering at London University before going to Switzerland to teach.

Although the government had pulled out of airships, Vickers were keen to develop commercial craft, and Barnes Wallis returned to work on the R100, designed to carry a hundred passengers. It was hoped that it would be able to reach India with just one stop in Egypt. He brought in many innovative features, and the R100 had a successful flight across the Atlantic.

Wallis later switched to aircraft design, applying some of the inventions he had used in airships to long range aircraft. He contributed to the design of the Wellesley bomber and later worked on the Wellington bomber, a phenomenal 12,000 of which were built. This was the main bomber in use during the Second World War until the development of the Lancaster.

By 1941, Barnes Wallis became convinced that it was necessary to attack the enemy at the heart of its industrial production. Initially, he wondered about dropping a huge bomb near to the Moehn and Eder dams in the Ruhr, sending shock waves through the earth to crack the dam walls. However, he soon realized that the bomb needed for such a task would have to be impracticably large.

It was at this stage that the seed of an idea began which was to lead to his most famous invention. He wondered if it would be possible to drop a bomb in the form of a spinning sphere that would ricochet across the surface of the water in a dam, and then sink and explode underwater close to the dam wall. After some initial experiments, he was able to convince Bomber Command that the idea was feasible, and his famous bouncing bomb was born.

BARNES WALLIS

The bouncing bomb was in fact a bouncing depth-charge, and tests led to its shape being changed from a sphere to a cylinder. Barnes Wallis found that if the cylinder was dropped in such a way that it rotated backwards, it would indeed bounce on the surface of the water. The main problem was to estimate where and when to drop it in order to ensure that the bomb would bounce up to the dam wall and then sink to a predetermined depth before exploding. The walls of the German dams each had two towers, which the British pilots would be able to use for sighting, but what was needed for practice runs was a British dam which resembled those in Germany.

There were two such dams in England, and these were in

Memorial stone at Derwent Dam. (David Moorley)

Derbyshire, Barnes Wallis's native county. Both the Derwent and Howden dams were built with two towers, and these would be perfect for the pilots of the dambuster squadron to perfect their techniques. Wing Commander Guy Gibson and his 617 Squadron practised over the Derbyshire reservoirs in March and April 1943. They were able to use a triangular device, which they sighted on the twin towers of the dam, to help them to calculate both the altitude and the distance from the dam at which to release their bombs.

The Derbyshire practice flights proved invaluable, and the dambuster raids on Germany in May 1943 were a big success. It is fitting that Derwent and Howden reservoirs played a part in this success, since the designer and prime mover of the whole idea was the Derbyshire hero Dr Barnes Wallis. According to Sir Henry Tizzard, the scientific adviser to Ministry of Aircraft production, Dr Barnes Wallis had 'made the finest individual technical achievement of the war'. He was awarded the CBE in 1943 and was knighted in 1968.

23

Peter Fidler

- 18th-century surveyor

Peter Fidler was born at Sutton Mill Farm in Bolsover in 1769. His father, James, was a farmer who also acted as the village constable, one of his duties being to supervise the village men who were required to spend a number of days each year maintaining the local roads.

As a boy, Peter loved to explore the north Derbyshire countryside around his home; this love of exploration was to last for the whole of his life. As well as enjoying the outdoor life, Peter certainly received a good education, not only learning to read and write but also studying mathematics and geometry. It is possible that he went to the Grange School at Hardwick Hall and even to Netherthorpe Grammar School, according to local historian K. Gordon Jackson. The same historian suggests that Peter's education may have been paid for by Lord Scarsdale, a local landowner.

His school studies were to stand him in good stead, when, at the age of nineteen, he enlisted to go to Canada as a labourer employed by the Hudson Bay Company. This company traded furs trapped in Canada by Europeans and native Americans. In exchange for the beaver and wolf furs, the company would trade knives, guns, powder and shot, beads, kettles, etc. Furs were in great demand in Europe, and so it was a thriving business.

When, in 1788, after eight weeks at sea, Peter arrived in Hudson Bay at the trading post named York Factory, he met

Philip Turnor, the surveyor to the Hudson Bay Company. Turnor was most impressed by the academic ability of the young man from Derbyshire and immediately upgraded him from labourer to clerk. It was not long before Peter and another young clerk, David Thompson, were made assistant surveyors.

At first, Peter accompanied Philip Turnor on his travels, but he was soon sent out alone to survey and record the huge blank parts on the maps, initially using just a compass and his knowledge of astronomy. Later, he was able to obtain and use a sextant and other navigational equipment. Over the next 30 years, Peter Fidler explored extensively throughout the north-west interior of Canada, travelling by canoe, by horse, by dog-sledge, and on foot, and all the while mapping previously unrecorded territory and making possible many new trade routes. One such was the 1,600 mile route from York Factory to Lake Athabasca and the Great Slave Lake. Peter Fidler is also credited with discovering coal at Drumheller, in western Canada, the existence of which was previously unknown.

He got on well with the native Americans, and for a while lived with the Chipewyan tribe, eating their food and dressing in the Indian manner, in deerskin and buffalo hide. He was amazed to find that there were over 30 different Indian nations; he learned to speak many of their 17 languages, which proved invaluable during his exploration and surveying. One Blackfoot chief, named Ackomoki, or 'The Feathers', helped Peter to map an unexplored area that included the upper Missouri river and the Rockies. Like all Peter Fidler's maps, they were sent by the Hudson Bay Company to both the Royal Society and the Admiralty in London, where they were published.

In 1794, at the age of 25, he met and fell in love with a young native American girl of the Cree nation. Her Cree

PETER FIDLER

Statue of Peter Fidler, carved from a redwood tree.
(Dick Richardson, Country Books)

name is unknown, but Peter always called her Mary, the same name as his mother. Mary bore him a son, Thomas, the following year, and another, Charles, in 1798. These were the first of their many children. In fact, during their 28 years together they had fourteen children, eleven of whom – seven boys and four girls – survived into adulthood. Unsurprisingly, Peter and Mary Fidler have many descendants still living in Manitoba and neighbouring parts of Canada. Their original marriage was a simple Cree ceremony, but, shortly before his death in 1822, Peter and Mary went through a formal church marriage.

There was always fierce competition between the Hudson Bay Company and other trading companies. The main rival was the North West Company, staffed largely by Scots, but there was also the smaller XY Company as well as many independent traders, who would try to poach the native fur trappers, persuading them to desert the Hudson Bay Company and transfer their dealings to them. At times, the rivalry would extend beyond mere dirty tricks to violence, arson, and even murder.

The secret weapon of the Hudson Bay Company was the fact that it had skilled surveyors like Peter Fidler. The North-Westers had to rely on the skills of one or two traders who knew the secret routes, but these were never written down and could not be followed by others. Peter was always a strong company man, and he was shocked when his friend and fellow surveyor David Thompson eventually left the Hudson Bay Company and went to work for the North West Company.

In 1811, Peter Fidler returned to his native Derbyshire on extended leave. His father had died and had stipulated in his Will that Peter would have to return to England within a year of his death. This may have been the prime reason for his return, but he was also keen to see his mother, sister, and brother. Once back, he set about having a new £400 house built for his mother, which he named Hudson's Bay House. He must have been missing the wildness of Canada; he certainly missed his lovely Mary and his children, and, when a letter came from the Hudson Bay Company asking him to return, he was not sorry to do so.

He returned to Canada less than a year after he had left and continued to work for the Hudson Bay Company until 1821. A year later, he died at Fort Dauphin, leaving a rich legacy of written accounts, maps, and meteorological charts. His written accounts describe life with the American tribes, watching Indians hunt a herd of buffalo by driving them over a cliff, and meeting a grizzly bear for the first time. In one passage, when he was ill, he complained of 'feeling badly', proving that you can take the man out of Derbyshire but never the Derbyshire out of the man! Just as he had named his mother's new house in Derbyshire Hudson's Bay House, many of the trading posts he founded in Canada were given Derbyshire names: Bolsover House, Chesterfield House, Sutton Mill, and he named one area Derwent after the Derbyshire river.

24

James Brindley

- canal builder who 'chained the seas together'

The village of Shardlow in south Derbyshire is as far from the sea as it is possible to get, and yet it was once a thriving port! That is because Shardlow was a canal port, where goods were taken from the narrow boats working the Trent and Mersey canal and loaded onto the wider barges used on the River Trent. Since the trans-shipment was not directly from one boat to another, warehouses were built to store the goods. Wharves were constructed to accommodate hundreds of boats being loaded and unloaded, and inlets leading to canal basins were excavated to provide access to the warehouses. At Shardlow, there were two specialized warehouses for storing salt and two for iron, though most of the others were for mixed use. A wide variety of goods was brought through Shardlow, including timber, coal, limestone, gypsum, cotton, pottery, malt, barley, and beer.

The inland port of Shardlow owes its existence to James Brindley, England's greatest canal builder. He was born in north Derbyshire, at Tunstead in the parish of Wormhill, near Buxton, in 1716. He was the son of a farm labourer, who liked to drink and gamble. James had little or no education and never learned to read or write. As a child, he worked as a crow scarer, rattling a tin of stones to keep the birds off the crops, and later as a wagoner taking corn to the local mill. Although no scholar, he was good with his hands and enjoyed making model mills out of wood, trying to make them work by wind or water power.

JAMES BRINDLEY

At 17, James was apprenticed to a millwright and wheelwright named Abraham Bennett. At first Bennett was dissatisfied with his new apprentice and threatened to send him home, but later he began to appreciate James's understanding of machinery. As he became more experienced, he was sent to fit or repair machinery at different locations. When Bennett died in 1742, James Brindley became a self-employed engineer and millwright at Leek. As well as fitting out the local silkmills and a papermill, he also developed a machine that could grind flints for Wedgewood, the pottery firm. He became interested in the use of engines to pump water out of flooded coalmines, thus adding another set of skills to his growing range. His ingenuity at solving engineering problems led to him being nicknamed 'Schemer', and his reputation spread.

When the Duke of Bridgewater wanted to build a ten mile canal to carry coal from his colliery at Worsley to the city of Manchester, he faced an almighty problem. The canal would have to cross the River Irwell. Needing advice, he sent for Schemer – James Brindley – who, despite his lack of knowledge of surveying, assured him it could be done by means of an aqueduct. Others were less sure. When a consultant engineer accompanied James to the site of the proposed aqueduct, he commented that although he had heard of castles in the air, this was the first time he had been taken to the place where one was to be constructed!

Nevertheless, the duke had faith in Brindley, and the aqueduct – 900 yards long, 12 yards wide, and supported on three massive stone arches – was built. From a mere castle in the air, it had become a wonder of the age, a tribute to one man's ingenuity and skill. People flocked to see the boats on the canal travelling high up over the river. This was 1761, and James Brindley was paid the princely sum of seven shillings a day. After the Bridgewater Canal was opened – and it will be noted that it was named after the proposer not the engineer – the price of coal in Manchester was halved as a result of the lower transport costs.

His second commission from the Duke of Bridgewater was the 24-mile Liverpool to Manchester canal. Then, in January 1766, a petition for a new canal was presented to parliament. This canal was to link the Bridgewater Canal to the River Trent, and was known as the Trent and Mersey Canal. However, James Brindley preferred the title The Grand Trunk Canal, as he saw it as England's main canal artery, from which all other canals would branch. Among its backers were the scientist Erasmus Darwin; the industrialist Josiah Wedgewood, who realized that the canal would come through the potteries; the Duke of Bridgewater; and

A former salt warehouse at Shardlow.

JAMES BRINDLEY

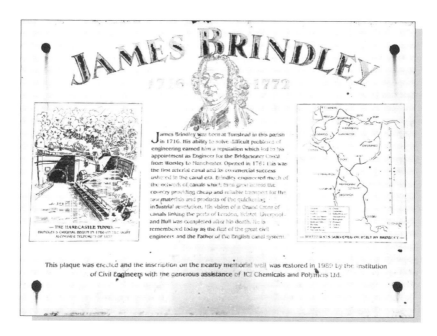

Monument to James Brindley at Wormhill. (David Moorley)

landowners and manufacturers from Derbyshire, Staffordshire, and seven other neighbouring counties. The Grand Trunk Canal took 11 years to build, and meant the construction of five tunnels and over 300 aqueducts. When it was finished, boats were able to travel between Liverpool, Hull, and Bristol by means of navigable waterways. It was a marvel of engineering on a huge scale.

The new canal passed through Shardlow, bringing about the establishment of this inland port. In 1975, the Shardlow Wharf Conservation Area was created, and many of the warehouses and other buildings relating to the canal have been conserved or restored, making Shardlow the best surviving example of an 18th century inland port.

In the north of the county, James Brindley also built the Chesterfield Canal, linking Chesterfield with the River Trent, via Worksop and Retford. He was paid a salary of £300 per annum for surveying and generally superintending the work, though he died before the canal was completed. Another engineer, John Varley, took over the construction work, and Hugh Henshall the surveying; obviously, it took at least two men to replace James Brindley, the Schemer.

At the age of 50, James Brindley had married Ann Henshall, a girl 30 years younger than he, but six years later, he died after getting a chill while surveying a canal in the pouring rain. He left two daughters from his marriage, and a natural son, John Bennett, born five years beforehand. The novelist Arnold Bennett was descended from this son.

Although the coming of the railways in the 19th century took much of the traffic from the canal system, commercial traffic was still using the canal at Shardlow in the 1950s. Brindley's memorial is the 350 miles of canals he left behind, linking together the Thames, the Humber, the Trent, the Severn, and the Mersey. In describing his achievements, it has been said that 'he chained the seas together'.

James Brindley certainly made his mark on his native Derbyshire, and at Shardlow his work is preserved for the present-day student of 18th century history and the canal enthusiast. There is also a drinking fountain at Tunstead, erected close to his birthplace as a monument to his memory. Each year it is dressed with flowers in the Derbyshire custom of well- and spring-dressing.

It is remarkable that this great pioneer remained unable to read and write. All his designs and plans were created not on paper but in his head. When he had a problem to solve, he was known to take to his bed for a day or two while he thought it out.

Bibliography

Bell, David: *Derbyshire Tales of Mystery and Murder*, Countryside Books, 2003

Bode, Harold: *James Brindley*, Shire Publications, 1973

Colquhoun, Kate: *A Thing In Disguise: Joseph Paxton*, Fourth Estate 2003

Daniel, Clarence: *Derbyshire Portraits*, Dalesman Pub. Co. Ltd, 1978

Durrant, David N.: *Bess of Hardwick*, Weidenfeld & Nicolson 1977

Eisenberg, Elizabeth: *Derbyshire Characters for Young People*, Hall & Sons Ltd, 1985

Eyre, Jim, and John Frankland: *Race Against Time*, Lyon Books, 1988

Green, Roger J.: *Catherine Booth*, Monarch 1996

Hall, Ian: *The Legends of Derby County*, Breedon Books, 2001

Innes-Smith, Robert (Ed.): *Derbyshire Characters*, Derbyshire Countryside Ltd, 1977

Jackson, K. Gordon: *True Brit: The Adventures of Peter Fidler of Bolsover*, Country Books, 2000

MacArthur, Ellen: *Taking on the World*, Penguin Books, 2002

Plowden, Alison: *Mistress of Hardwick*, BBC Publications, 1972)

Rippon, Anton, and Andrew Ward: *The Derby County Story*, Breedon Books, 1998

Robinson, Brian (Ed.): *The Seven Blunders of the Peak*, Scarthin Books, 1994

Smith, Mike: *Derbyshire Canals*, J.H. Hall & Sons Ltd, 1987

Snelling, Stephen: *Passchendaele 1917*, Sutton Publishing, 1998

Acknowledgements

I would like to thank Ashby Design + Print, Jo Baines, Michael Baines, Simon Brooks, Barry Brown, Jeff Clifton, Sheila Cook, Jim Eyre, G.H. Gill, Martyn Gillie, Hazel Greaves, Jack Holland, Jean and David Moorley, Graham Nutt and Graham Foster of Magic Attic in Swadlincote, T. Payne, Bronwen Quarry of the Hudson Bay Co. Archives, Dick Richardson of Country Books, Winifred Redfern, Dennis Skinner MP, Joyce Smith, Nigel Vardy, Jonathan Wallis of Derby Art Gallery, and Eric Walton.